KING'S
TREASURY
OF
DYNAMIC HUMOR

KING DUNCAN

SEVEN WORLDS PRESS,
P.O. Box 11565, Knoxville, TN 37939

Dedicated to my four daughters for whom I am profoundly grateful.

When small, they laughed at Daddy's jokes;
As teenagers, they groaned, then told them to their friends.

Table of Contents

Achievement

After striking out in a game, Charlie Brown pours out his heart to Lucy: "I'll never be a big-league player! I just don't have it! All my life I've dreamed of playing in the big leagues, but I know I'll never make it!"

Lucy replies, "You're thinking too far ahead, Charlie Brown. What you need to do is to set yourself more immediate goals. Start with the next inning, for example. When you go out to pitch, see if you can walk out to the mound-- without falling down."

Someone asked me if I ever realized any of my childhood dreams. I answered that I had. When my mother used to comb my hair, I often wished I didn't have any.

There was an unusual story on radio station WGN awhile back. A fellow sat down and ate 874 Walleye minnows at one sitting. That's a lot of Walleye minnows! Why did he do such a strange thing? Because earlier in his life he had sat down and eaten 862 Walleye minnows and his accomplishment was listed in the *GUINNESS BOOK OF WORLD RECORDS.* So he set out to break his own world record--and he did! But he was disappointed when he sent in his new world record to the Guinness people. They told him that his new record would not be listed in the upcoming editions of the *GUINNESS BOOK OF WORLD RECORDS*, nor will his old one. It seems that they have a new policy; from now on no records will be listed which might be considered hazardous to a person's health!

Zig Ziglar tells of visiting the Washington monument. As he and his party approached the monument, he heard a guide announcing loudly that there would be a two-hour wait to ride the elevator to the top of the monument. However, with a smile on his face the guide then said, "There is no waiting to go to the top if you are willing to take the stairs."

In the *PEANUTS* cartoon, the team "statistician" brings Charlie Brown, the manager, his report. "I've compiled the statistics on our baseball team for last season," Linus says. "In 12 games we ALMOST scored a run and in 9 games the other team ALMOST didn't score before the first out. In right field, Lucy ALMOST caught 3 balls and once ALMOST made the right play."

"We led the league," he concludes, "in 'almosts,' Charlie Brown."

A certain priest, an avid football fan, had to hear confessions during an important Nebraska-Oklahoma game. When one man had finished confession, the priest asked him, "Are you by any chance going to be around awhile?"

"Yes, Father," answered the man. "I'm painting the church and I'll be here all afternoon."

"Would you mind then," the Father asked, "coming back in now and then and keeping me posted on the game?"

"Sure," the man said.

Later, the priest slid open the confessional grille, and heard, "Father, my last confession was fifteen minutes ago. Since then I ain't done nothing, and neither has Nebraska."

Snoopy, the cherished *PEANUTS* cartoon pet, sat droopy-eyed at the entrance of his dog house. He lamented, "Yesterday I was a dog. Today I'm a dog. Tomorrow I'll probably still be a dog. SIGH. There's so little hope for advancement!"

Action

Some of you are *GARFIELD* fans. In one of his cartoons he is shown resting droopy-eyed in his bed thinking to himself: "One of my pet peeves," he says to himself, "is people who never finish what they start." As he cracks a knowing smile, he says, "I do not happen to be one of those people." The last frame shows him under the bedcovers saying, "My philosophy is, 'Never start anything.'"

A very bashful young man was hesitant about demonstrating his affection for his sweetheart. "Oh, but that I were an octopus," he said one night, "that I might wrap all eight arms around you." His impatient sweetheart replied, "Don't worry about having eight arms. Just make better use of the two arms you already have."

A certain little lad wanted to spy on his sister and her new beau. He knew they liked to sit under a certain tree, so before the young suitor arrived, the little boy climbed high up in the tree and hid himself.

Soon he heard the amorous young couple down below. The fellow was evidently trying to make his first advance and impress the girl at the same time. He looked up at the night sky and said with a loud voice, "Little star up above, should I kiss the girl I love?" Boy, was he surprised when he heard a voice from above answer, "Sixteen-year-old down below; pucker up and let her go!"

Civil War General McClellan was a genius at dithering--finding a million ways to keep from doing what had to be done.

So President Lincoln sent this message to him: "If you haven't any plans for the Army of the Potomac, would you mind lending it to me for awhile?"

Brian Harbour tells a great story about a group of animals in the jungle who decided to have a football game. The problem was that no one could tackle the rhinoceros. Once he got a head of steam, he was unstoppable. When he received the opening kick-off, he rambled for a touchdown. The score was seven to nothing immediately. Somehow, they managed to keep the ball away from him the remainder of the first quarter. At the beginning of the second quarter, the other team tied the score 7 to 7. The lion tried to warn the zebra on the kick-off not to kick it to the rhinoceros. But the zebra ignored the warning. The rhino caught the ball and there he was racing for the touchdown. Suddenly, out of nowhere, he was brought down with a vicious tackle. When the animals unpiled, it was discovered that a centipede had made the tackle. "That was fantastic!" congratulated the lion. "But where were you on the opening kick-off?"

The centipede replied, "I was still putting on my shoes."

A certain fisherman was enormously successful. Each morning he would take his small boat out on the lake and within a few hours he would return with a boat loaded with fish. People wondered, how did he do it?

One day a stranger showed up and asked the man if he could go along the next time the man went out fishing. The man said, "Sure. Meet me here tomorrow morning at 5:00 and we will go out." The next morning the two of them made their way through the early morning mist to a small cove where the fisherman stopped the boat and cut off the motor. The stranger wondered where the man's fishing equipment was. He had no rod and reel. All the stranger saw was a small net and a rusty tackle box.

Slowly the man pulled the tackle box over to himself, opened it, and took out a red stick of dynamite. Taking a match, he lit the fuse of the dynamite, held it for a moment and heaved it into the water. There was a terrific blast. Soon he was dipping up fish in his small net and filling up the boat. After watching this the stranger reached into his hip pocket and pulled out his wallet. Opening it up, he flashed a badge --the badge of a game warden. Somberly he said, "You're under arrest." This didn't seem to rattle the fisherman in the least. He reached into the tackle box, pulled out another stick of dynamite, lit it, held it for a moment while the fuse burned on down, then handed it to the game warden. "Now," he said, "Are you just going to sit there or are you going to fish?"

Once the eminent philosopher John Dewey found his son in the bathroom. The floor was flooded and he was mopping furiously trying to contain the water in that room, keeping the damage to a minimum. The professor began thinking, trying to understand the deeper ramifications of the situation. After a few moments, the son said, "Dad, this is not the time to philosophize. It is time to mop!"

Somewhere I read about some aspiring psychiatrists who were attending their first class on emotional extremes.
"Just to establish some parameters," said the professor, "Mr. Jones, what is the opposite of joy?"
"Sadness," said the student.
"And the opposite of depression, Ms. Smith?"
"Elation."
"How about the opposite of woe, Mr. Brown?"
"I believe that's giddyap," the student replied.

Comedian Sam Levenson says his father came to America because people told him the streets were paved with gold. When his pop arrived, he found that not only were the streets not paved with gold, but they weren't paved at all, and everybody expected him to do the job.

During the Nazi occupation of Paris, a husky storm trooper stepped into a subway car and tripped headlong over the umbrella of a little old lady sitting next to the door. After picking himself up, the bruised Nazi launched into a tirade of abuse, then bolted from the car at the next station. When he was gone, the passengers burst into spontaneous applause for the little old woman. "I know it isn't much," she said, graciously accepting the compliments, "but he's the sixth one I've brought down today."

Two Kentucky farmers who owned racing stables had developed a keen rivalry. One spring, each of them entered a horse in a local steeplechase. Thinking that a professional rider might help him outdo his friend, one of the farmers engaged a crack jockey. The two horses were leading the race at the last fence, but it proved too tough for them. Both horses fell, unseating their riders. But his calamity did not stop the professional jockey. He quickly remounted and won the race. Returning triumphant to the paddock, the jockey found the farmer who had hired him fuming with rage. "What's the matter?" the jockey asked. "I won, didn't I?"

"Oh, yes," roared the farmer. "You won all right, but you still don't know do you?"

"Know what?" asked the jockey.

"You won the race on the wrong horse!" ∞ Herb Miller, *Actions Speak Louder Than Verbs,* (Nashville: Abingdon Press, 1989).

*A*DVERSITY

Some boy scouts from the city were on a camping trip. The mosquitoes were so fierce, the boys had to hide under their blankets to avoid being bitten. Then one of them saw some lightning bugs and said to his friend, "We might as well give up. They're coming after us with flashlights."

In a recent cartoon strip, *ZIGGY* is in open ski country. He is carrying a book and he is accompanied by his dog. He says to the dog, "We won't get lost hiking in the woods this time because I brought the cross-country skier trail guide book...

"Matter of fact, Fuzz, this area here looks none too familiar. I better consult the guide.

"See, there are three methods of finding our way home. First, there's the 'coin flip method.' I think we'll skip that....

"Two is the eeny-meeny-miney-mo method! Uh....that doesn't sound too good....Ah, here we go!!

"Three: 'The auditory method.' Sounds impressive, doesn't it? Let's see what it says to do.

"A. Get comfortable. B. Take a deep breath. C. Yell 'Help' as loud as you can!'"

In one *PEANUTS* cartoon Charlie Brown was at the beach carefully building a castle in the sand. Standing back to admire his work, he was soon engulfed by a downpour which leveled the castle. Standing before the smooth place where his artwork had once stood, he said: "There must be a lesson here, but I don't know what it is."

From *BORN LOSER,* one man says, "Know what I admire most about you, Chief? Your sky-diving hobby! How in the world did you ever get started on that?"

"WW II...The engine on my P-51 Mustang died."

An army rookie had just arrived at an army training camp. The lad was curiously inspecting the livestock at too close range, when one of the mules kicked, knocking the boy cold. His buddies got him on the rebound, placed him on a stretcher and started for the infirmary. Regaining consciousness, the rookie felt the swaying motion of the stretcher, and, cautiously lowering his hand over the side, felt only space.

"Gosh," he moaned in horror, "I ain't hit ground yet!"

In his book *A SCENT OF LOVE*, Keith Miller tells an hilarious but true story about a mother who took her children to the Animal Farm. This was a place where they could pet animals that roamed free. They could even ride an elephant. The parking lot was full when they arrived, so Mom parked their little red Volkswagen bug on a little pathway that led away from the ranger station. Then they went out and had a great time.

The day went quickly. Suddenly Mom remembered they were supposed to pick up Dad that evening at the airport. Since it was nearly evening already she hurriedly gathered the kids and rushed to the parking lot. There they made a startling discovery. In her words, "The front end of the car was just smushed."

The mother was furious. She stalked up to the ranger station, and banged on the door. Before she could speak, the man at the desk said, "Lady, I'll bet I know who you are. You're the owner of the little red Volkswagen. Don't worry, the Animal Farm will pay for your repairs. But let me explain what happened." He explained that Millie, the Animal Farm elephant was trained in the circus to sit on a little red tub. "When Millie saw your car," explained the ranger trying to stifle a laugh "she couldn't resist. But we are going to fix it."

The car was still driveable since Volkswagen motors are in the rear. More time had elapsed, however, and Dad would be waiting at the airport. On to the freeway Mom and the kids zoomed in the little "smushed" Volkswagen. This was definitely not their day, though. Down the road aways they encountered a long line of backed-up traffic, obviously caused by a wreck.

Mom was getting desperate. She whipped the little red bug onto the shoulder of the freeway and started making her way around the line of cars. She didn't even notice the two patrolmen on motorcycles at the accident site. One was writing while the other was directing traffic. The first officer looked up and saw this little smushed-up red car speeding away from the accident. He ran to his motorcycle, turned on his siren and gave chase. When he pulled her over he said, "Look, lady don't you know it is against state law to leave the scene of an accident?" She replied, "I wasn't involved in any accident." He raised his eyebrows and looked at the front of her car and asked, "What happened to your car?" She replied, "An elephant sat on it."

That is when the officer brought out a little balloon for her to breathe into. ∝Keith Miller, *The Scent of Love*, (Waco: Word Books, 1983).

During a railroad strike in England, a volunteer engineer on the one line performed the remarkable feat of bringing the train to his destination 25 minutes ahead of time.

The passengers went forward in a body to thank him. A pale face emerged from the cab. "Don't thank me," he gasped. "Thank God. I only found out how to stop this thing ten minutes ago!"

Sometimes it is hard to get our act totally together. Somewhere I read a story about a concert held in Philadelphia. One of the movements featured a flute solo that was to be played as if coming from a distance. The conductor had instructed the flutist to stand offstage where he was to count the measures precisely in order to come in at the exact time, since there could be no visual contact between the conductor and the soloist. On the performance night when the time came for the flute solo, the flutist began exactly. The fine, lilting notes floated out beautifully. Then suddenly there was a pinching sour note and the soloist was silent for the rest of the piece. The conductor was outraged and at the end of the piece he rushed off stage to find the poor flutist. The player was prepared. "Maestro," he said, "before you say anything let me tell you what happened, but really, you're not going to believe it. You know I came in accurately, and everything was going beautifully, when suddenly--this enormous stage hand ran up, grabbed away my flute, and pushed me back, saying, "Shut up, you idiot! Don't you know there's a concert going on out there?"

Comedian Harpo Marx loved to shock strangers with his zany antics. He was at the Pasadena train station to see a friend off and noticed two elderly women seated in the dining car. On impulse, Harpo rushed onto the train, seized the menu and tore it up and devoured it.

Unperturbed, one woman turned to the headwaiter. "Please let us have another menu," she said. "Someone has eaten ours." ∽ Oscar Levant, *The Unimportance of Being Oscar* (Putnam)

There is a story about a monastery in Europe perched high on a cliff several hundred feet in the air. The only way to reach the monastery was to be suspended in a basket which was pulled to the top by several monks who pulled and tugged with all their strength. Obviously the ride up the steep cliff in that basket was terrifying. One tourist got exceedingly nervous about half-way up as he noticed that the rope by which he was suspended was old and frayed. With a trembling voice he asked the monk who was riding with him in the basket how often they changed the rope. The monk thought for a moment and answered brusquely, "Whenever it breaks."

On one of the jungle-cruise boat rides at a certain theme park a nervous lady passenger asked the guide if he ever had trouble with snakes dropping into the open boat from overhanging limbs.

"Naw," he drawled, "no trouble. You got a snake in the boat, then you got people in the water. You got people in the water, you got alligators in the water. You got alligators in the water, you got people back in the boat. Ain't no trouble at all."

Jed and Myrtle were a frontier couple. They had recently homesteaded a new place. They built a cabin and a barn and settled in with their few livestock fairly comfortably. Then Jed hung a big bell in a tree. He explained, "That's for emergencies, Myrtle. There are hostile Indians hereabouts. You ring that bell if you are in danger."

Sometime later Jed was out in the fields doing some work. Suddenly he heard the bell ring. He headed home at full gallop.

"What's wrong?" he asked.

"I just thought maybe you'd like some cool water," Myrtle said.

Jed was fit to be tied. He stressed to Myrtle that water was not an emergency. He still had work to do.

He rode out to check a section of fence he was putting up. Again he heard the bell. Again he raced home.

"The fire was getting low," said Myrtle and she thought he might want to tend to it.

"That ain't no emergency!" said Jed. "Don't ring that bell until something really urgent comes along."

Two hours later Jed heard the bell ring again. He charged home to find the cabin in flames. The barn had burned to the ground and his few cattle were long gone. Myrtle was slumped against the house with an arrow in her shoulder. "Now, Myrtle," Jed exclaimed, "this is more like it!"

Henry Kissinger, when secretary of state, is reported to have looked at his calendar and told an aide, "There cannot be a crisis next week. My schedule is already full."

In a little town in Georgia, a motorist had to pay a farmer $20.00 to pull him out of a mud-hole. "Seems to me that you'd be so busy pulling folks out of these lousy mud roads that you'd be doing it day and night."

"Nope. Cain't pull em' out at night," drawled the farmer. "Night's when we tote water to muddy the road!"

In 1916, Georgia Tech University in Atlanta played a football game against Cumberland University, a tiny law school. The Tech team was a mighty football powerhouse and rolled over Cumberland by a score of 222 to 0. Needless to say, Tech also pretty well beat the Cumberland players to a pulp.

Toward the end of the game, Cumberland quarterback Ed Edwards fumbled a snap from center. As the Tech linemen charged into his backfield, Edwards yelled to his backs, "Pick it up! Pick it up!" Edward's fullback, seeing the monsters rush in who had battered him all day, yelled back, "Pick it up yourself--you dropped it." ∞ Fred Russell, *I'll Try Anything Twice* (Nashville, TN: The McQuiddy Press, 1945), p. 17.

William H. Hinson tells about an amusing article that appeared in his local paper. Over the past several years in Houston, Texas, there have been a rash of incidents in which dogs have attacked small children. As a result, the newspapers have run several stories about the attacks--some of which have been pretty gruesome. There was one, however, involving a little boy called D.J. that was not so tragic.

A reporter asked D.J. how he managed to come away from a recent dog attack unharmed. You can almost picture the serious expression on the little guy's face as he said, "Well, right in the middle of the attack, the Lord spoke to me."

"Oh, really," asked the reporter, "And what did God say?"

"He said, 'Run, D.J., run!'" the young man reported.

Deep in our hearts we agree with Lucy in the *PEANUTS* cartoons when she says, "I don't want ups and downs. I want ups and ups and ups!"

A third grade teacher had been working long and hard to help a certain student improve his behavior and attitude. After a reading session that was continuously disrupted by this student, the teacher in her frustration said to the boy, "John, I am going to turn you over to God."

Another boy who happened to be walking by said, "Mrs. Jones, God is going to give him right back to you."

I like the story of the little boy who was taken to the dentist. It was discovered that he had a cavity that would have to be filled. "Now, young man," asked the dentist, "what kind of filling would you like for that tooth?" "Chocolate, please," replied the youngster.

Many of you are familiar with the airlines' Frequent Flyer programs. The various bonus mileage programs that airlines devised in the 1980s to foster customer loyalty have had some strange fallout. Many companies have denied their employees private benefits from such programs, after discovering that they were sometimes flying the most roundabout routes in order to get more mileage. A rather extreme example of going out of one's way to qualify for bonus coupons came when TWA flight 847 was hijacked in June, 1985, and was flown four times between Algeria and Beirut. Larry Hilliard, regional director of corporate communications for TWA, revealed that Deborah Toga, wife of one of the hostages, had inquired whether these hostage trips qualified under the airline's Frequent Flyer program. They did.∽Peter Hay, *The Book of Business Anecdotes*, (New York: Facts on File Publications, 1988).

I got a chuckle when I read about something that happened to Prince Charles and Lady Di on their visit to Australia and New Zealand. Walking freely among the crowds in South Australia, the princess made for a group of young children, the nearest of whom she patted affectionately on his tousled head. "Why aren't you at school today?" she inquired. "I was sent home," the lad replied, "because I've got head lice."

A novice sailor asked a veteran skipper how he learned the positions of Chesapeake Bay's many shoals and bars. The reply: "Hit 'em all."

During a hectic field campaign in Europe, General Dwight Eisenhower is said to have asked one of his intelligence officers for a brief assessment of the enemy situation. The young officer quickly replied, "Sir, picture a donut. We're the hole!"

A man was riding in a taxi when he realized he had left his wallet at home. Suddenly he had an idea. About a block away from his destination, he said to the driver, "Stop at this hardware store and wait for me. I need to buy a flashlight so I can look for the hundred dollar bill that I dropped back here." When the man came out of the hardware store, the taxi was gone.

Ed Meese, the former attorney general had a memorable way of putting it. This will be especially meaningful to football fans. Meese recalls the advice of his predecessor, William French Smith, who warned Meese that there would be many a day in his new position when he would feel like "the javelin competitor who won the toss of the coin and elected to receive."

Former President Ronald Reagan likes to tell a story, which he says is true, about a newspaper photographer out in Los Angeles who was called in by his editor and told of a fire that was raging out in Palos Verdes, a hilly area south of Los Angeles. His assignment was to rush down to a small airport, board a waiting plane, get some pictures of the fire, and be back in time for the afternoon edition.

Breathlessly, he raced to the airport and drove his car to the end of the runway. Sure enough, there was a plane waiting with the engines all revved up, ready to go. He got aboard, and at about five thousand feet, he began getting his camera out of the bag. He told the fellow flying the plane to get him over the fire so he could take his pictures and get back to the paper. From the other side of the cockpit there was a deafening silence. Then he heard these unsettling words: "Ah...Aren't you the instructor?"

*A*DVERTISING

In Mark Twain's early days as the editor of a small Missouri newspaper, he once received a letter from a reader who had found a spider in his paper. He wrote asking if this was an omen of good or bad luck.

Replied Twain: "Finding a spider in your paper is neither good luck nor bad. The spider was merely looking over our paper to see which merchant was not advertising so that he could go to that store, spin his web across the door, and lead a life of undisturbed peace ever afterward."

Doing business without advertising is like winking at a girl in the dark. You know what you're doing but nobody else does.

Effective advertising is like playing the cymbals. A little boy attended his first symphony concert. He was excited by the splendid hall, the beautiful people in all their formal finery, and the sound of the large and enthusiastic orchestra. Of all the instruments in the orchestra, however, his favorite was the cymbals. The first loud, dramatic crash of those brass disks won him over without reservation. He noticed, though, that most of the evening the cymbal player stood motionless while the other musicians played on. Only occasionally was the cymbal player called upon to make his contribution and even then his time of glory was quite brief.

After the concert the little boy's parents took him backstage to meet some of the musicians. The little fellow immediately sought out the cymbalist. "Say, mister," he asked sincerely, "How much do you need to know to play the cymbals?" The musician laughed and answered, "You don't have to know much at all. You only have to know when."

Thomas Jefferson, like any author, did not like the idea of a committee making revisions to his marvelous Declaration of Independence. His friend, Benjamin Franklin, comforted him with a little story. When he was a young man, Franklin said, he had a friend who was about to open up a hatter's shop. He composed a sign with the inscription "John Thompson, Hatter, makes and sells hats for ready money" over the depiction of a hat. He showed it to his friends and asked them what they thought.

The first one remarked that "Hatter" was superfluous, as "makes and sells hats" showed the nature of the business. The second pointed out that "makes" could be left off the sign, as customers were unlikely to be interested in who had made the hats. The third friend said that as it was not the custom locally to sell on credit, the words "for ready money" were superfluous, and they too were struck out, leaving just: "John Thompson sells hats."

"No one would expect you to give them away," said the fourth friend, "so what is the point of 'sells?'"

Finally, someone said that it seemed unnecessary to have the word "hats" on the board, since there was the painted picture of a hat. So the board eventually read "John Thompson" with a picture of a hat underneath the name.

Franklin's story mollified Jefferson, and it was generally agreed that the committee's editorial work had improved the wording of the Declaration of Independence. ⌘*The Little Brown Book of Anecdotes*, Clifton Fadiman, General Editor (Boston: Little, Brown and Company 1985).

When F.W. Woolworth opened his store, a merchant down the street ran an ad in the local paper. It read: DO YOUR LOCAL SHOPPING HERE. WE HAVE BEEN IN BUSINESS FOR FIFTY YEARS! Woolworth countered with an ad of his own. It read: WE'VE BEEN IN BUSINESS ONLY ONE WEEK -- ALL OF OUR MERCHANDISE IS BRAND-NEW!

$\mathcal{A}$GE

An elderly lady was driving a big, new expensive car and was preparing to back into a parallel parking space when suddenly a young man in a small sports car zoomed into the space--beating her out of it. The lady charged out of her car and angrily demanded to know why he had done that when he could easily tell she was trying to park there and had been there first. His response was simply, "Because I'm young and I'm quick." When he came back out a few minutes later, he found the elderly lady using her big new car as a battering ram, backing up and then ramming it into his parked car. Now he was very angry and asked her why she was wrecking his car. Her response was simply, "Because I'm old and I'm rich."

The prospect for life insurance was filling out the necessary application. To the question that asked for the applicant's weight, the man filled in "189--with glasses." The insurance representative was puzzled by this unusual entry. "Why don't you put down your weight minus the glasses?" he asked.

"Because I can't read the bathroom scales without them," the applicant replied.

"Forty isn't old - if you're a tree!"

You've all seen those tags hanging in automobile windows, like "Child on board." I saw one awhile back which said: "Childish adult at the wheel."

One lady told how her family gathered around the television to witness the arrival of Pope John Paul II when he visited this country. As they watched the Pontiff step from the plane and symbolically kiss the ground, her 80-year-old aunt turned to her and confided, "I know just how he feels. I hate to fly, too."

Aunt Dosia, who married a parson, retained a faint beauty in her old age, but time took its toll in other ways. Once at the Easter Communion, when her husband handed her the full chalice, she drained it to the last drop, murmured, "Perfectly delicious," and handed it back in the presence of the whole congregation. ∞ Shane Leslie, *Long Shadows*

A man had just had his annual physical exam and was waiting for the doctor's initial report. After a few minutes the doctor came in with his charts in his hand and said, "There's no reason why you can't live a completely normal life as long as you don't try to enjoy it."

A lady turned to her husband and said, "Charles, remember all those things we said we'd never live to see? Well, we're seeing them now--on T.V." ∞ *Mature Living Magazine*, January 1988

When the Roman statesman Cato set out to learn the Greek language at eighty years of age, his friends could only laugh and ask how could he contemplate such a lengthy course of study at his advanced age. Cato replied that it was the youngest age he had left.

According to George Burns: "You know you're old when your favorite part of the newspaper is '25 Years Ago Today'; when you stoop to tie your shoelaces and ask yourself, 'What else can I do while I'm down here?' and when everybody goes to your birthday party and stands around the cake just to keep warm."

A young man asked: "Pop, when does old age start?"
"It can start at any age, depending on the individual," said the father, smiling. "But actually, old age is the time when you find yourself giving good advice instead of setting a bad example."

> ### "HOW TO KNOW WHEN YOU'RE GETTING OLDER:
>
> *Everything hurts and what doesn't hurt, doesn't work!*
>
> *Your little black book contains names ending in 'M.D.'*
>
> *You get winded playing chess.*
>
> *You turn out the lights for economic reasons rather than romantic.*
>
> *You sit in a rocking chair and can't get it going.*
>
> *Your knees buckle and your belt won't.*
>
> *Dialing long distance wears you out.*
>
> *Your back goes out more than you do.*
>
> *You walk with your head held high, trying to get used to your bifocals.*
>
> *You look forward to a dull evening.*
>
> *You don't care where your wife goes, just so you don't have to go along.*

An archaeologist is the best husband a woman can have; the older she gets, the more interested he is in her. ∞ Agatha Christie (who married one)

Doctor: You're as fit as a fiddle, you will live to be 80."
Patient: "But I'm already eighty."
Doctor: "See, what did I tell you?"

"Old refrigerators never die, they just lose their cool."

As the three ladies picked up the menus, each put on a pair of glasses. "Of course, I really need mine only for close reading," remarked the first. "I only wear mine when the light is poor," explained the second. The third was much franker. "I rarely wear mine," she declared, "except when I want to see!"

Groucho Marx once questioned a woman on his television show: "How old are you, ma'am?" asked the comedian, never one to hold back on such matters.

"I'm approaching forty," she said, with a little reluctance.

"Approaching forty?" responded Groucho. "From which direction?"

A secretary was telling her office mates about her birthday party.

"You should have seen the cake," she boasted. "It was marvelous. There were twenty-three candles--one for each year."

"Twenty-three," said a colleague cattily. "What did you do, burn them at both ends?"

A friend of mine says: "Getting old doesn't mean you can't chase girls. The only change may be that you have to chase them downhill."

President Reagan told a joke at a White House reception. It seems that an 80-year-old man's golf game was hampered by poor eyesight. He could hit the ball well but he couldn't see where it went. So his doctor teamed him up with a 90-year-old man who had perfect eyesight and was willing to go along to serve as a spotter. Here's how the columnist reported the dialogue after the 80-year-old man hit the first ball and asked his companion if he saw where it landed:

"Yep," said the 90-year-old.

"Where did it go?" the 80-year-old demanded.

"I don't remember," the 90-year-old replied.

It was New Year's Day at Pete's house. His grandfather, a man ninety-four years of age was there and so were many of the old gentleman's sons and daughters, grandsons and granddaughters, and even great-grandsons and great-granddaughters. It was quite a crowd, to be sure.

The bowl games were on television. Children were playing with their Christmas toys. The ladies were trying to rest from the meal preparation and housecleaning, and the men were wandering from the television to the scraps of turkey and boxes of chocolates. Perhaps it was just a typical Christmas, first year, family reunion.

The grandfather's heart was weak, and so he wore a pacemaker, a small battery-powered device, that helps prolong the life of many people. Halftime had come to the football game, and the old gentleman was left alone in front of the television.

That's where the real story begins. The band was performing on the football field, and the lovely majorettes were tossing their batons into the air. Pete happened to be standing behind his grandfather, his presence undetected. When the cameraman provided a closeup shot of one of the beautiful girls, Pete said, "Granddad was sitting on the edge of his chair tapping his pacemaker and saying, 'Don't go out now! Don't go out now!' He was hanging in there." ∞ Jerry Hayner, *Yes, God Can,* (Nashville, Tennessee: Broadman Press).

I like to jog at a local high school track, so I enjoyed hearing a middle-aged man's story about his jogging experience. He was puffing around the track that circled the high school football field while the team was practicing. When the players started running their sprints up and down the field, he told himself, "I'll just keep running until they quit." So they ran. And he ran. And they kept running. And he kept running. Finally, in exhaustion he stopped. An equally exhausted football player walked past the jogger and said, "Boy, I'm glad you finally stopped, mister. Coach told us we had to keep running wind sprints as long as the old guy was jogging!" ∞ Ken Durham, *Speaking from the Heart,* (Ft. Worth, Texas: Sweet Publishing, 1986).

Somewhere I heard about an elderly gentleman who had a variety of health problems. His hearing was going as well as his sight. Arthritis kept him in constant pain. Complaining to his pastor he said, "I don't know why God just doesn't take me on home!" His pastor, trying to reassure him answered, "God must still have something for you to do." The old man snapped, "Well, I'm not going to do it!"

When the over-70 Ronald Reagan was campaigning for the presidency, an 80-year-old woman said to him, "Everything you said sounds fine. But what about us old folks? Haven't you forgotten us?" Mr. Reagan smiled and said, "Forgotten you? Heavens, how could I ever forget you? I am one of you."

One lady tells how, after years of persuasion, her mother was finally talked into having a cataract operation. Returning home from the hospital, the mother sat down in front of the picture window, which looked out onto a lake.
"Do you notice any difference in the view, Mom?" the daughter asked.
"I certainly do," her mother replied. "Don't you ever dust?"

I try to remember the case of the gentleman who went in for a physical examination and then said to the doctor, "Okay. Give it to me straight. I can take it." And the doctor said, "Let me put it to you this way. Eat the best part of the chicken first."
∞ Ronald Reagan

ANGER

When Narvaez, the Spanish patriot, lay dying, his father-confessor asked him whether he had forgiven all his enemies. Narvaez looked astonished and said, "Father, I have no enemies, I have shot them all."

We're like the woman who was bitten by a mad dog, and it looked as if she were going to die from rabies. The doctor told her she had better make her will. Taking her pen and paper she began to write; in fact she wrote and wrote.

Finally the doctor said, "That is surely a long will you're making."

She snorted, "Will nothing! I'm making a list of all the people I'm going to bite!"

Whenever I get angry, I close my eyes and count to ten. I was mad at my brother while driving on the expressway and closed my eyes. The next thing I knew there was a terrible crash. ∞ Brian Herbert, *Incredible Insurance Claims,* (Los Angeles: Price/Stern/Sloan Publishers, Inc., 1982).

Someone has said, "Speak when you're angry--and you'll make the best speech you'll ever regret."

Heinrich Hein once wrote, "My nature is the most peaceful in the world. All I ask is a simple cottage, a decent bed, good food, some flowers in front of my window, and a few trees beside my door. Then if God wanted to make me wholly happy, he would let me enjoy the spectacle of six or seven of my enemies dangling from those trees. I would forgive them all wrongs they have done me--forgive them from the bottom of my heart, for we must forgive our enemies. But not until they are hanged!"

He who loses his head usually is the last one to miss it. ∞ Anonymous

Edith in television's *ALL IN THE FAMILY*: "I worry more about Archie getting worried...cause he don't know how to worry without getting upset."

Evangelist Sam Jones was chided for hitting a man.

"Why did you do it?" asked a friend.

"Well," said Sam, "The Bible says to turn the other cheek when someone strikes you. A man hit me and I turned the other cheek. And after that I hit him back. The Bible doesn't tell us what to do after we have turned the other cheek, so I hit him."

There is a humorous story about professional golfer Tommy Bolt. On the golf course Bolt was known for two things--his graceful swing and his terrible temper. Many stories are told about his quirky temperment. Once, after missing six straight putts, generally leaving them teetering on the very edge of the cup, Bolt shook his fist at the heavens and shouted, "Why don't you come down and fight like a man!"

A man with a terrible temper was playing a round of golf with his pastor. After leaving three straight putts on the edge of the cup the man exploded. "I missed!" he screamed. "How could I miss?" With that he heaved his putter into a nearby lake, kicked a wheel on the golf cart and drove his fist into a nearby tree. His pastor was shocked. "I have never seen such a terrible display of anger," he said to the poor man. "Don't you know that God doesn't like us when we are angry? You better watch out. I have heard that there are angels whose one assignment is to search out people who express their anger so ferociously and to send a lightning bolt from the heaven to burn them to a crisp." The man was embarrassed and better behaved the next few holes. However, on the last three holes his putter failed him again. When the last putt veered off to the right just in front of the hole, the man went crazy. "I missed!" he screamed in despair. "How could I miss?" He broke his club across his knee and threw it as far as he could, he kicked up several large clumps of dirt on the edge of the green and once more drove his fist into a nearby tree. All of a sudden the sky grew dark as an ominous cloud passed over. There was a clap of thunder and an awesome burst of lightning--and the pastor was burned to a crisp! An eerie silence filled the golf course. All that could be heard was a quiet voice from heaven: "I missed! How could I miss?"

When one of the hostages was interviewed after his release he was asked if he would ever go back to Iran. He replied, "Yes, in a B52 bomber."

$\mathcal{A}$PATHY

You remember the Smothers Brothers? Several years ago, they did a routine on TV that went something like this:

Dick asked, "What's wrong Tommy? You seem despondent."

Tom replied, "I am! I'm worried about the state of American society!"

Dick said, "Well, what bothers you about it? Are you worried about poverty and hunger?"

"Oh, no, that doesn't really bother me."

"I see. Well, are you concerned about the possibility of war?"

"No, that's not a worry of mine."

"Are you upset about the use of illegal drugs by the youth of America?"

"No, that doesn't bother me very much."

Looking puzzled, Dick asked, "Well Tom, if you're not bothered by poverty and hunger, war and drugs, what are you worried about?"

Tommy replied, "I'm worried about apathy."

A bumper sticker bore the sign, "America's Greatest Problem is Apathy--But Who Cares?"

George Carlin said a few years ago: "Scientists have just discovered a cure for apathy. However, no one has shown the slightest interest."

APPEARANCE

Did you hear about the movie company that put up a movie set on a highway in California? Part of the set was a false filling station. The filling station looked so realistic that people passing by would stop their cars to buy gas. A couple of stage hands decided to have a little fun when the cameras weren't running. Whenever an unsuspecting motorist would pull up to the false station, the stage hands would act like they were filling the car with gas. Then they would tell the motorist that because of a special promotion the gas that day was free. The motorist would drive out of the station with a big smile on his face that probably stayed there right up until the moment she or he ran out of gas.

APPRECIATION

A brawny man stood in front of a painting by the great artist Sargent in an art gallery in New York City. He kept muttering to himself, "I've been given a place at last. I have a place at last." Artist Robert Henri was standing nearby. Henri was mystified at the man's words. "Are you in this sort of work?" he asked the man.

"Oh, yes," said the man, "but this is the first time I've been displayed like this."

Now Henri really was disturbed. "But I thought that this work was by the great painter Sargent," he said.

"That's right," said the man, "but it was me that made the frame."

A man went fishing one day. He looked over the side of his boat and saw a snake with a frog in its mouth. Feeling sorry for the frog, he reached down, gently took the frog from the snake, and set the frog free. But then he felt sorry for the snake. He looked around the boat, but he had no food. All he had was a bottle of bourbon. So he opened the bottle and gave the snake a few shots. The snake went off happy, the frog was happy, and the man was happy to have performed such good deeds. He thought everything was great until about ten minutes passed and he heard something knock against the side of the boat. With stunned disbelief, the fisherman looked down and saw the snake was back with two frogs!

*A*TTITUDE

Lucy stands with her arms folded and a resolute expression on her face, while Charlie Brown pleads, "Lucy, you MUST be more loving. This world really needs love. You have to let yourself love to make this world a better place in which to live!"

Lucy whirls around angrily causing Charlie Brown to do a backwards flip and screams at him: "Look, blockhead--the *WORLD* I love. It's *PEOPLE* I can't stand."

In the cartoon *BEETLE BAILEY* sometime back, a soldier is moving through the chow line. Strangely enough he is complimenting the cook and he asks, "How do you keep track of how everyone likes his eggs?" The cook answers, "By personality...Sarge likes his eggs hard boiled... The Chaplain gets his sunny side up."

A middle-aged woman was in a bookstore. She was in a foul mood and was taking it out on one of the clerks. She accused him of never stocking the books she wanted to read and always being out of the current best sellers. The poor clerk, trying to maintain his composure, asked her, "Well, what is the title of the book you wish to purchase?" She answered, "*HOW TO REMAIN YOUNG AND BEAUTIFUL.*" The clerk, with a sarcastic smile on his face answered, "Very well, I will place your order for *HOW TO REMAIN YOUNG AND BEAUTIFUL* at once--and I will mark it urgent."

I like the attitude of a college student down at Ft. Lauderdale, Florida, who was thrown in jail with some of his friends for partying too zestfully during the Easter holidays. "I demand my constitutional right to make one phone call," he said to the police sergeant.Fifteen minutes later a delivery boy called at the jail. "Who ordered a combination pizza with everything?" he asked.

An old New England farmer cleared his land of the rocks that covered it. With those rocks he built a rock fence that was three feet high and four feet wide. When someone asked him why the unusual dimension, three feet high and four feet wide, he said that he built it that way so that if the wind blew the fence over it would be taller than ever before.

A man was in a bar. Hoping to strike up a conversation with a distinguished looking fellow sitting nearby, he said, "May I buy you a drink?"

"No," said the man coolly, "Don't drink. Tried it once and I didn't like it."

"Would you like a cigar?"

"No. Don't smoke. Tried tobacco once and I didn't like it."

"Would you like to join me in a game of gin rummy?"

"No. Don't like card games. Tried it once, and I didn't like it. However, my son will be dropping in after a bit. Perhaps he will join you."

The first man settled back in his chair and said, "Your only son, I presume?"

A certain lady was full of miseries. Her pastor came by to see her one day and she began her litany: "The neighbor's children are so noisy...People at the church never come to see me...my arthritis is getting worse...the weather has been so terrible..." On and on she went with one complaint after the other. Finally she said, "But do you know, Pastor, I have had the worst headache all week, but suddenly it has disappeared." The pastor sighed and said, "Oh,no. Your headache didn't disappear. I have it now."

A man approached Horace Greeley one day to ask for a donation for foreign missions.Greeley turned him down but the man continued his plea and Greeley again said no. Finally the unfortunate one said: "Why, Mr. Greeley, wouldn't you give $10 to save an immortal soul from going to hell?"

"No," shouted Greeley, "not half enough people go to hell now!"

John Wesley, founder of the Methodists, and a friend were forced to sleep on a floor,using their coats for pillows for several weeks while on a preaching assignment. After nearly three weeks of this spartan life, Mr. Wesley awakened one morning about three o'clock.Turning over, he clapped Nelson on the side and said, "Brother Nelson, let us be of good cheer. I have one whole side yet, for the skin is off but one side!"

Some of you will remember when Clyde Beatty was the most famous lion tamer in the world. While Beatty was performing with THE GREATEST SHOW ON EARTH he also operated a small circus that played during the off-season. This circus was stationed in Fort Lauderdale, Florida, and, due of the very favorable climate from December through March,performed in the open air, without a big-top. One day there was a heavy downpour and Beatty was forced to call off the show. Only one person had come to the box office to buy a ticket--a little old lady with a big umbrella and a bigger voice. When she was told that the performance had been cancelled, she asked to see the manager. When he appeared she told him that she had paid her money and insisted on seeing the show. When he tried to refund her money, she refused it.

The manager called for Beatty. The little lady was growing more adamant all the time. She explained to Beatty that tomorrow she would be returning to Indiana. She had tried several times, she said, to catch the circus when he would be appearing with his lions but had missed him each time before. She had heard on the radio that the circus performed rain or shine, and she asserted that she was not leaving without seeing a complete performance. Beatty was left speechless. This had not been a light sprinkle. Water was everywhere. Like the manager, he tried to return the lady's money, but she would have none of it. She was so insistent, so adamant, that finally Beatty caved in. (It is amazing how a man who can go into a cage of lions can be intimidated by one little, elderly lady.)

The show went on in spite of the downpour. Beatty's performers were furious with him. Imagine performing their acts and dodging pools of water. Imagine the time it took the clowns to put on their make-up to perform for an audience of one--and then to feel that make-up smear in the steady downpour. Even his animals seemed to have a look of disgust on their faces, according to Beatty. The elephants loved the mud, but their keeper had to spend hours afterwards hosing them down. The whole experience was one miserable mess. Of course, they had to make some unannounced cuts here and there, but finally they got through an entire performance, and Beatty felt pretty good about it. He had given the little lady what she asked for--even if he had alienated all his performers in the meantime. ☞ Clyde Beatty, *Facing the Big Cats* (Garden City, NY: Doubleday & Company, Inc. 1984).

BIBLE

Loyal Jones and Billy Edd Wheeler in their hilarious book, *LAUGHTER IN APPALACHIA,* (New York: Ivy Books, 1987) tell a great story about a country preacher who announced that he would preach on Noah and the Ark on the following Sunday.

He gave the scriptural reference for the congregation to read ahead of time. A couple of mean boys noticed something interesting about the placement of the story of the flood in the Bible. They slipped into the church and glued two pages of the pulpit Bible together.

On the next Sunday the preacher got up to read his text. "Noah took himself a wife," he began, "and she was..." He turned the page to continue, "...300 cubits long, 50 cubits wide and 30 cubits high." He paused, scratched his head, turned the page back and read it silently, turned the page and continued reading. Then he looked up at the congregation and said, "I've been reading this old Bible for nigh on to fifty years, but there are some things that are hard to believe."

When Daniel Webster, the 19th century statesman and orator, was a young boy, he was zealous to read and learn. The only book available to him at that point was the Bible. As he lay in bed reading his Bible one night, he accidentally managed to set the covers on fire. In response to a strong scolding, he explained, "that he was in search of light, but was sorry to say that he received more of it than he desired."

One little fellow turned to a classmate and asked, "Who was Round John Virgin?" She answered, "I think he was one of the 12 opossums."

When my son Stephen was still a preschooler, we were traveling in the car when he introduced a statement with the exclamation, "Holy cow!" I took this opportunity to remind him that only God and His things are holy. He nodded his four-year-old agreement, and finally concluded with the observation, "But you can say holy Scriptures, can't you Dad, 'cause the Bible's God's Word?" I assured him he could, and on we drove, I happily convinced I had taught an important theological truth to my son. About ten minutes later came an excited shout: "Holy Scriptures, Dad--look over there!" ∞ Gary Inrig, *A Call to Excellence,* (Wheaton, Illinois: Victor Books, 1985).

During family devotions we often quiz our children about biblical accounts to help them learn. When we asked Carey who built the ark, the gleam in her eye told us she knew the answer.

"Noah," she answered with authority.

Turning to Tim, we asked who in the Bible had said, "I am that I am." (Exodus 3: 14) He wrinkled his forehead and squinted as he searched for the answer. Then his eyes opened wide.

"Popeye!" he fairly shouted with pride. ∞ Chris Werley, Mason, Ohio: in CHRISTIAN HERALD

*B*USINESS

Norman Vincent Peale tells about a business executive who had three boxes on his desk labeled *INCOMING, OUTGOING, and UNDECIDED.* The latter usually contained the most papers. Then he added a fourth box which he labeled *WITH GOD ALL THINGS ARE POSSIBLE.*

Some of you can sympathize with the owner of a small motel in a sparsely populated area in the southwest. A recent graduate of a prestigious business school, eager to show off his new knowledge, was staying in the motel.

"How's business?" he asked the owner.

"Not very good," the tired looking man answered.

"Well, what's your next step?" asked the business major. "What's your plan to rectify the situation?"

"Well," said the owner drily, "I've never made enough in this business to stick with it, but I've never lost enough to get out of it. I'm hoping to do one or the other this year."

Someone once said, "Distrust first impulses. They are nearly always right." And another has said, "Don't look before you leap. If you do, you will decide to sit down."

There's a story about a fellow who was employed by a duke and duchess in Europe.

"James," said the duchess to this employee, "how long have you been with us?"

"About thirty years," he replied.

"According to my records," said the duchess, "you were employed to look after the dog."

"Yes, Ma'am," James replied.

"James, that dog died twenty-seven years ago."

"Yes, ma'am," he said. "What would you like me to do now?"

I believe that fellow used to work for us!

There is a parable about a king who ordered his wise men to condense all human wisdom into one memorable phrase. They returned after twelve years of work with twelve volumes. "It is too large," protested the king. "Condense it further!" So the wise men returned in a year and presented one large volume in place of the twelve. "It's still too large," protested the king. They went out again, only to return the following day with a single statement written on a slip of paper--all the world's wisdom in one line: There is no free lunch.

William Henry Jackson was one of the first to photograph some of nature's most majestic scenes in the American Southwest. His work, done in the late 1800's, required the laborious transporting of 120 pounds of cameras, plates, chemicals, and a dark-tent up steep mountainsides and across the rugged western terrain. In many instances, Jackson could get only his camera and tripod to the exact spot from which he made his photographs. He then had to climb from dark-tent to camera and back again for every photographic plate he made. Ten developed plates in a day was considered good, and 15 plates was exceptional.

Jackson lived on into the age of 35-mm cameras, automobiles, and airplanes. However, he had a tendency to assess progress in terms of the goals for which he himself had invested such hard work. Upon seeing his first automobile, Jackson remarked, "What a fine way to get around with a camera!"

There was a sign on a plant manager's door: "If you have problems, come in and tell me about them. If you don't, come in and tell me how you do it."

There was once a farmer who had two mules. One was named Willing and the other was named Able. However, Willing was willing but was not able. Able was able but was not willing. The farmer did not get much done.

In his book *DATELINE AMERICA*, Charles Kuralt tells of a sign he saw on the door of a cafe in Indiana. It said: Open 24 hours a day, 7 days a week. Closed Thursday.

The founder of McDonald's, Ray Kroc, was asked by a reporter what he believed in. "I believe in God, my family, and McDonald's," he said. Then he added, "When I get to the office, I reverse the order."

A woman had ordered a book from a large publishing company. Several weeks later she received the following letter: "Many thanks for your recent order. We wish we could fill it at once, but improvements in our procedures will mean a delay in shipping."

Murphy's Law--"*IF ANYTHING CAN GO WRONG, IT WILL*"--should be extended as follows: "*AND USUALLY LATE ON A FRIDAY AFTERNOON.*"

"No matter how tired you may be, your exhaustion is fully justified, as can be proven by simple arithmetic. The U.S. has a population of 200 million. Of these, 72 million are over 65 years old, leaving 128 million to do the work. When you subtract the 75 million people under 21, you get 53 million. There are also 24 million employed by the Federal Government, which leaves 29 million to do the work. The 12 million in the Armed Forces leave only 17 million to do the work, and, when you subtract from this the 15,765,000 who are in state and city offices and 520,000 in hospitals, mental institutions and similar places, the work force is reduced to 715,000. Fine, but--462,000 are bums and vagrants, leaving only 253,000 to do the work. There are 252,998 people in jail, leaving--you guessed it--just 2 people, you and me. And I'm getting tired."

"The only person who behaves sensibly," said George Bernard Shaw, "is my tailor. He takes new measurements every time he sees me. All the rest go on with their old measurements."

An efficiency expert looks at a symphony orchestra playing an unfinished symphony by Schubert:
1. For considerable periods, the four oboe players had nothing to do. Their number should be reduced, and their work spread over the whole orchestra.
2. Forty violins were playing identical notes. This seems unnecessary duplication, and this section should be drasti-

cally cut. If a larger volume of sound is required, this could be achieved through an electronic amplifier.

3. Much effort was absorbed in the playing of demi/semi-quavers. This seems an excessive refinement, and it is recommended that all notes be rounded to the nearest semi-quaver. If this were done, it should be possible to use trainees and lower-grade operators.

4. No useful purpose is served by repeating with horns the passage that has already been handled by the strings. If all such redundant passages were eliminated, the concert could be reduced to twenty minutes.

If Schubert had attended to these matters, he probably would have been able to finish his symphony after all.

∞ Harry Mackay, *Swim with the Sharks Without Being Eaten Alive* (New York: William Morrow and Co., Inc., 1988).

Sign in a hot dog stand near the bus garage in West Hollywood, California: "*BUS DRIVERS MUST HAVE EXACT CHANGE*"

A factory worker was called on the carpet by the manager for talking back to his foreman.   "Is it true that you called him a liar?" asked the manager.

"Yes," said the worker, staring down at the floor.

"Did you call him stupid?"

"Yes."

"Slave driver?"

"Yes."

"And did you call him an opinionated, bull-headed egomaniac?"

The fellow looked up questioningly. "No. . .should I have?"

In a *SMART CHART* Cartoon, two businessmen are gazing at a sales chart with the line off the chart headed toward the basement. Says one to the other: "If we could just get back up to broke, we could quit."

An industrial expert went around asking different people, "What do you like best about your job?"

"The good pay," one factory worker replied.

"What do you like least about your job?" asked the expert.

"The good pay," he said again.

The expert was surprised. "What do you mean? You like it the best and you like it the least?"

"Well, I like it because it pays me well, so that's the good part. But if it didn't pay so well, I'd quit! That would be better!"

John Pelley was the head of the American Association of Railroads. He used to be with the Illinois Central Railroad. John left the Illinois Central and went over to the Central of Georgia, just at the time the depression hit. It was pretty bad. He got there just at the wrong time, and he began to have to make a lot of cuts.

Times were bad, so Pelley began to do everything. He would take the porters who had been on the private cars, working two days a week, and he would make them do other jobs, and they would have to go out on runs which they didn't like. In fact, he began to fire everybody, and it got very, very bad.

Pelley said he walked down to his office one morning and on his way, overheard two of the porters talking.

The first porter said, "Boy, I dreamed last night that this fellow Pelley died."

The other said, "He did?"

The first porter said, "Yes, and I went to the funeral."

"What happened then?"

"Well, they were bringing the casket down the aisle, when all at once they threw the top of the casket up and Mr. Pelley stuck his head up and said, 'How many pallbearers?' Somebody said, 'Eight,' and Mr. Pelley said, 'Let two go.'"

Here is a story that says a lot about customer service. A man was preparing his favorite breakfast of hot oatmeal when his daughter came rushing in with his little grandson.

"The baby-sitter has been delayed," she explained, "and I've got to go to work. Will you keep Bobby for a few hours?"

Granddad said sure and his daughter left. Then Granddad scooped up two bowls of oatmeal. "Do you like sugar?" he asked.

When Bobby nodded he asked, "How about some butter, too?"

When his grandson nodded again he asked, "How about milk?"

"Sure," the boy said.

But when the grandfather placed the steaming bowl of oatmeal in front of Bobby, the boy made a face and pushed it away.

"But when I asked you, you said you liked sugar, butter and milk," grandfather protested.

"Yeah," Bobby answered, "but you didn't ask me if I like oatmeal."

In *WHAT THEY DON'T TEACH YOU AT HARVARD BUSINESS SCHOOL,* author Mark McCormack shows how one businessman made his point by suggesting an obviously foolish idea:

Many years ago, the Ford Motor Company went through a period in which the accountants literally took over the company and were closing plants left and right in order to cut costs. They had already succeeded in shutting down plants in Massachusetts and Texas and seemed to be relishing their newly found power.

Robert McNamara, who was president of Ford at the time, called a meeting of his top executives to discuss a recommendation he had received for the closing of yet another plant. Everyone was against it, but the predictions from the accountants were so grim that no one was willing to speak up.

Finally, a salty Ford veteran by the name of Charlie Beacham said, "Why don't we close down all the plants and then we'll really start to save money?"

Everyone cracked up. The decision was made to postpone any more closings for a while, and the "bean counters" went back to working for the company rather that running it.

Lucy: I'm thinking of starting some new hobbies...

Charlie Brown: That's a good idea, Lucy. The people who get the most out of life are those who really try to accomplish something.

Lucy: Accomplish something?! I thought we were just supposed to keep busy!

One morning, the offices of IBM headquarters were covered with the admonition: *THINK.*

The next morning the walls of the offices bore an additional sign beneath the other one: *OR THWIM.*

CELEBRITY

Fred Allen once quipped that a celebrity is one who works to be known, then wears dark glasses so as not to be recognized.

Tip O'Neill tells a great story on himself. O'Neill had a chance encounter with a man while waiting in an airport not too long ago. After a few minutes the man said to O'Neill, "Say, you don't recongize me, do you?" "No, I really don't think so," said the senator. "You see, I'm so well known. I have this big shock of white hair and this large red nose, and I'm on the TV news two or three times a week. A lot of people recognize me, but I can't kept track of all the people I meet. Who are you?" The man answered, "We met at a dinner party about six weeks ago in Washington. My name is Robert Redford."

Fitness expert Jack LaLanne declares that he may never die. "It would wreck my image," he explains. "I can't even afford to have a fat dog." ∽ *Time*

CHANGE

Change is always difficult. I am reminded of the little old lady who stood up at a lecture that Dr. Werner Von Braun was giving and said to the good Doctor, "Why can't we forget about all these new-fangled ideas about going out into space and be content to stay at home and watch television like the good Lord intended?"

Two men were living on a houseboat. One night, while the men were sleeping, the boat broke loose from its mooring and drifted into the open sea. One of the men got up in the morning before his mate and, going out on deck, noticed there was no land in sight anywhere. Excitedly, he called to his mate, "Joe, get up quick; we ain't here any more!"

Some people have a theme song: "Come well or come woe, my status is quo."

Comedian Henny Youngman tells about the time he was thrown out of an antique shop. "All I did," he said, "was walk in and ask, 'What's new?'"

One of the mistakes we make in life is the assumption that things will remain as they are. I am reminded of a little story about Peter Jenkins of *WALK ACROSS AMERICA* fame. Peter Jenkins searched all over America for the perfect place to relocate a few years back. He wanted to get away from the noise and pollution of urban life. He chose a quiet community, Spring Hill, Tennessee. Nothing much happens in Spring Hill--a lovely community near Nashville.

At least nothing much happened in Spring Hill until a couple of years ago--after Peter Jenkins had already located there. General Motors announced it was building a gigantic new auto plant for their forthcoming Saturn automobile. Where? You guessed it--Spring Hill, Tennessee. Land prices have sky-rocketed. Tremendous growth has been projected for the entire area. You can run but you can't hide!

Character

I recall the story of a man's funeral. The wife and her two sons were seated on the front pew. The songs had been sung and the preacher began to elocute about the departed brother:

"He was a man's man." "Amen," said the congregation.

"He was a man who worked hard." And a few said "Amen."

"He was a man the bottle could not control."

"Amen," said one or two mourners.

"He was a man who loved his home and wife and children."

"Amen."

"He was a man who paid his debts and a man who told the truth." (No amens.)

The poor wife could stand it no longer, so she told one of her sons, "Joe, go up and look in the casket and see if that's your daddy he's talking about."

One old fellow died. He had always been a scoundrel. He was mean to his wife, and neglected his children. He had never darkened the door of the church. They had a graveside service.

The local Baptist pastor performed the service. People wondered what the good pastor would say about him. Finally the big moment came and he faced the congregation and said, "Well now, beloved, you know he wasn't as bad all the time as he was most of the time!"

When Ulysses S. Grant discussed why he voted for James Buchanan over John C. Fremont in 1856, he simply said, "I knew Fremont."

Will Rogers once said, "Live in such a way that you would not be ashamed to sell your parrot to the town gossip."

Years ago three young men in the Bible Belt were caught red-handed breaking the Sabbath. Guilt-ridden for their sins and fearful of the punishment they were likely to receive, they stood before their stern pastor. They shook with fear as he asked for an explanation of their behavior.

The first young man, feeling great guilt, said, "Sir, I was absent-minded and forgot that yesterday was the Sabbath."

"That could be," replied the pastor. "You are forgiven."

Also very upset, the second young man said he too was absent-minded. "I forgot that I was not allowed to gamble on the Sabbath," was his excuse.

"Well, that could also be," said the pastor. "You are forgiven."

Finally the pastor turned to the young man in whose home these events occurred. "Well, what is your excuse? I suppose you were absent-minded, too!"

"I sure was, sir," said the lad, a known troublemaker and the instigator of the card game. "I forgot to pull the shades down!"

CHILDREN

Mark Twain once wrote: "A soiled baby, with a neglected nose, cannot be scientifically regarded as a thing of beauty."

Even though children are deductible, they can also be very taxing.

The floorwalker of a department store discovered a little fellow standing near an escalator with his eyes glued upon the moving handrail. "Something wrong, sonny?" asked the floorwalker. "Nothing to worry about," the boy assured him. "I'm just waiting for my chewing gum to come back."

One minister was teaching a fifth grade Sunday School class about the life of John. He told how John had lived in the wilderness with little or nothing to eat. He commented that John had eaten only honey and locusts. A little girl asked what locusts are. The minister said, "A locust is a grasshopper." The little girl said, "Oh, my grandmother drinks those."

- Taking care of your baby is easy, as long as you don't have anything else to do.

Dear Mama:
Having good time, I think. We take long hikes. Send my other sneaker.

Your son

Give me 200 active two-year olds and I can conquer the world. --Anonymous

No one is thirstier than the child reluctantly gone to bed.

I was reading about a young mother who was a full-time homemaker but who was still having difficulty coping with a 3 year old, a 1 and 1/2 year old and a new born baby. Her husband came home one day to find five dozen diapers hanging on a line in the back yard. "I saw all the white flags in the back yard," he said sympathetically. "I take it that you have surrendered."

Two little boys had turned their tree house into a space station. Their lively imaginations had them fighting Star Wars all over again. Suddenly the mother of one of them stood beneath the tree and shouted, "Johnny Jones, you come home right now." One of the little fellows said sheepishly to the other, "Uh, oh! I believe I hear earth calling."

You may have heard about the mother who was laboring in the kitchen, preparing a special recipe for supper. Her little boy was giving her fits--running in and out of the kitchen and ignoring his mother's threats and warnings. When he finally knocked the special dish off the table, his mother grabbed a broom and started after him. When he crawled under the house, she decided to let her husband take care of the boy. When he arrived home from work, she yelled, "Go discipline your son! Do something about your son!" The father crawled under the house looking around, until he saw two bright eyes peering around a pillar, and heard a soft voice say, "Dad, is she after you too?"

I love the story about the Sunday School teacher who was trying to teach the Ten Commandments to her young students. She thought it would be most helpful if she used some concrete illustrations. "Early one Saturday morning Johnny's parents were going shopping," she read to them. "They asked Johnny to wash the dishes while they were gone. When they returned, however, Johnny was watching cartoons and the dishes still were unwashed." In one accord the class responded, "Honor thy Father and Mother!"

"Good," said the teacher. "Ann went shopping with her mother but when no one was looking, she slipped a candy bar into her pocket." Again, the class was quick: "Thou shalt not steal!"

"Great," said the teacher. "Andy was a cruel little boy and had a bad temper. He got angry with his little sister one day and, grabbing her pet kitten, he threatened to pull its tail off." Now this was a much tougher example. Everyone was real quiet for a moment but then one little fellow brightened up and shouted, "What God hath joined together let no man put asunder!"

One little fellow was asked who it was who went into the den of lions and survived.

He thought for a moment and replied confidently. "It was Tarzan."

A Sunday School teacher asked her class who the first man was. A little boy answered, "George Washington." She then informed him that the first man was Adam. The boy responded, "Oh, well, if you are speaking of foreigners, maybe he was."

There was a delightful story many years ago in *TOGETHER* magazine in which a five-year-old girl was asked by the minister how many children there were in her family.

She replied, "Seven."

The minister observed that so many children must cost a lot.

"Oh, no," the child replied. "We don't buy 'em, we raise 'em."

Nancy Burns of Charlotte, North Carolina, tells in the *CHRISTIAN HERALD* about teaching a Sunday School class of 5-year-olds and asking if anybody could tell where to find the Ten Commandments.

The blank stares amid silence were filled by a freckle-faced cherub who said very seriously, "Have you looked it up in the Yellow Pages?"

A cartoon shows two boys walking to school, discussing their parents. One of them says to the other one, "I've figured out a system for getting along with my Mom. She tells me what to do and I do it."

Two theologians were walking across a seminary campus when one asked the other, "Do you believe in Original Sin?" The other said, "Yes, I do. We have a child." "Do you believe in Total Depravity?" asked the first man. "No, I don't. That is an excess of Calvinistic theology," replied the second.

The first replied, "Just wait until you have two children!"

There was once a man who was trying to read the evening newspaper after he had come home from a rough day at the office. As he attempted to read the paper, he was constantly being interrupted by his children. One child came and asked for money for an ice cream cone, and his father gently reached into his pocket and gave him the necessary coins. Another child arrived in tears. Her leg was hurt and she wanted her daddy to kiss the hurt away. An older son came with an algebra problem, and they eventually arrived at the right answer. Finally, the last and youngest of them all burst into the room looking for good old dad. The father said cynically, "What do you want?" The little youngster said, "Oh, daddy, I don't want anything. I just want to sit on your lap."

Once, while affectionately joking with our three-year-old daughter Maria, I asked her, "Where did we get such a nice girl like you?" She replied, "Jesus gave me to you."

I persisted, "But why did He give you to us, and not to somebody else?" She thought a moment, then quite confidently blurted, "Cuz my clothes are here!" ☞Ben and Karen Lewans in *Catholic Digest*

Old time proverbs do not apply to this modern world according to some 4th grade students at St. George's Episcopal Day School in Clarksdale, Miss.:

"A penny saved...buys one piece of gum." (Heather Franklin)

"Where there's a will...there's a greedy son." (Amanda Daho)

"If you can't stand the heat...hop in the pool." (Tucker Dearman)

"People who live in glass houses...don't take baths." (Charles Flower) ☞Contributed

Little Johnny came home from Sunday School and told his mother that if he missed three Sundays in a row, the teacher would throw him into the furnace. The horrified mother telephoned the teacher at once. "What I said was," the calm teacher explained, "that if any child missed three Sundays in a row, he would be dropped from the register." ☞*Presbyterian Life*

A father took his small son to visit the family's new arrival in the nursery of a country hospital. From the large window where he stood, the boy could see 15 tiny cribs in which 13 babies lay.

"Oh, look, Daddy!" he exclaimed. "They have two more traps set."

The modern child quizzed her mother as to her origin, and was given the traditional answer, "God sent you."

"And how did you get here, Mother? Did God send you too?"

"Yes, dear."

"And grandma?"

"Yes, dear."

"And great-grandma?"

"Yes, dear."

"Do you mean to say, Mother, that there have been no normal births in this family for over a hundred years?"

A *FAMILY CIRCUS* cartoon depicting children returning from Bible class: "We learned the fourth commandment: 'Humor thy father and thy mother.'"

As the salesman came to the front door, he turned to the little boy sitting on the steps and asked, "Is your mother home?" The boy said, "Yes," and the salesman began to ring the doorbell. After several rings and no response, the salesman looked down at the little boy and said, "I thought you said your mother was home." The tike looked up innocently and replied, "My mother is home, but this is not my home."

I don't want to sound like an old fuddy-duddy, but I know children get confused when we layer the holiest of seasons with fantasy (No, I don't want to get rid of Santa Claus). However, I can appreciate the frustration of the Sunday school teacher who was working with her primary group. "Do you know who Matthew was?" she asked.

When she received no answer she asked, "Do any of you know who Mark was?" Still no answer.

"I'm sure that somebody knows who Peter was," she said. "Can anyone tell me please, who was Peter?"

A little boy raised his hand and said, "I think he was a wabbit."

Father to son, looking at his report card: "Your grades don't promise much of a future, but your conduct marks indicate that you've already had quite a past!"

The mother of three notoriously unruly youngsters was asked whether or not she'd have children if she had it to do over again.

"Sure," she replied, "but not the same ones. ☞*Capper's*

A mother held her three-year-old son on her lap and informed him that he would soon be a big brother. She said that he could push the baby's carriage, hold the baby's bottle, and help by bringing her diapers. The lad wriggled out of his mother's lap and with his hands on his hips, said seriously, "What are *YOU* going to be doing while I do all the work?"

"My son collects stamps--a very educational hobby," the doting mother boasted to her neighbor. "Just listen: Kevin, tell us where Hungary is."

"Two pages in front of Italy," came the prompt reply.

September is when millions of shining, happy faces turn toward school. They belong to mothers.

After the kids leave home, some parents suffer from the empty-nest syndrome; others change the locks.

A teacher was telling her second graders about Abraham Lincoln.

"When he was your age," she said, "he lived in a little log cabin in the country, and every day he had to walk six miles to the schoolhouse."

Came a shout from the back of the room, "Crazy kid kept missing the bus, huh?" ∞ Taken from *The Woodman of the World Magazine,* June, 1988

A schoolboy turned in the following history essay: "It was Nathan Haley who said, 'I regret that I have but one life to give for my country.' This has come to be known as Haley's comment."

A new boy from way up in the hills came to school. He was eager to learn and asked questions about everything he saw.

In the new school he saw some electricians at work.

"What are those men doing?" he asked his teacher.

"They are putting in an electric switch."

The boy started up in alarm.

"I'm going back to the hills," he exclaimed. "I won't stay in a school where they do the switching by machinery."

On Maundy Thursday we have sometimes re-enacted the Last Supper and concluded with a dramatic presentation on the seven last words. A wooden cross is used in the baptistry with a pale blue light and wailing music from "The Soul of Israel." As each of the seven words is spoken, the light dims and goes out on the words, "It is finished." Then a storm arises with thunder and flashes of lightening, silhouetting the cross. Following the storm the music brightens and the light gradually floods the cross again.

I showed this one Easter to our nursery school children at the church. A couple of weeks later our neighbor, who was a Presbyterian, told me, "Branan, you'll get a charge out of this." They had Communion and their son, Alan, kept asking, "Daddy, what's that?" "Be quiet, and I'll tell you when we get outside." So after the service Alan wanted to know, and his father told him the bread and wine represented the body and blood of Jesus. Alan looked rather puzzled, so his dad said "You know how Jesus died, don't you, Alan?" To which the boy replied rather cockily, "Sure, Rev. Thompson showed us all about it. He got struck by lightening." ∽Branan Thompson, Colonial Avenue Baptist Church, Roanoke, Va.

A little boy had been named after his father. One day his mother answered the phone and a child's voice asked to speak with George.

"Do you want little George or big George?" she asked.

"I think I want big George," was the reply, "you know, the one in third grade."

Arriving for a visit, the woman asked her small granddaughter, "Megan, how do you like your new baby brother?"

"Oh, he's all right," the child shrugged. "But there were a lot of things we needed worse." ∽*Modern Maturity*, June-July 1987

CHRISTMAS

In a *FAMILY CIRCUS* cartoon, the little girl sits her baby brother on her lap and tells him the story of Christmas. According to her version, Jesus was born just in time for Christmas up at the North Pole surrounded by eight tiny reindeer and the Virgin Mary...Then Santa Claus showed up with lots of toys and stuff and some swaddling clothes...The three wise men and the elves all sang carols while the Little Drummer Boy and Scrooge helped Joseph trim the tree...In the meantime, Frosty the Snowman saw this star...

In a *CHARLIE BROWN* Christmas special, Charlie Brown just couldn't get into the Christmas spirit. Thus his little friend Linus observed: "Charlie Brown, you're the only person I know who can take a wonderful season like Christmas and turn it into a problem."

In a *PEANUTS* cartoon strip Charlie Brown is reading the Christmas story: "In those days a decree went out from Caesar Augustus that all the world should be enrolled." Charlie pauses and turns to Maurice to explain, "Caesar Augustus was the Emperor of Rome and the most powerful person on earth! One night in the little town of Bethlehem, a child was born, but no one paid any attention...After all, he was born in a common stable. Who would have thought that this child one day would be revered by millions while Caesar Augustus would be almost forgotten?" Peppermint Patti interrupts and says, "No one paid any attention when I was born either, but now everyone loves me, and I'm gonna get so many presents for Christmas, it'll make your head swim!"

Charlie Brown turns to leave, Bible closed, and Peppermint Patti says, "Hey! Aren't you gonna finish the story?" Charlie Brown replies, "I think you finished it..."

There was a cartoon not long ago picturing three little boys coming to the manger scene bearing gifts. The first two boys brought traditional gifts representing the gold and frankincense. The third little boy, however, came to the baby Jesus with a very large box of disposable diapers! Mary could only have wished! Someone, though, in that cartoon had captured love made practical.

One of my favorite *PEANUTS* cartoons has Lucy coming to Charlie Brown and saying, "Merry Christmas, Charlie Brown. Since it's this time of the season, I think we ought to bury past differences and try to be kind." Charlie Brown asks, "Why does it just have to be 'this time of the season'? Why can't it be all year long?" Lucy looks at him and exclaims, "What are you, some kind of fanatic?"

In *ZIGGY* the little boy sits on Santa Claus' lap and says: "Naughty and nice?! Boy--talk about limitations!"

Cartoonists often put things more succinctly than preachers. They have limited space to "speak" and get to "the bottom line" quickly. For instance, this social comment from *SHOE*:

Skyler: "What was it you wanted for Christmas, Uncle Cosmos?"

Uncle Cosmos: "I told you, Skyler, just a little peace and quiet."

Skyler: "I know, but I just came from the mall. I think they're out of it."

Back in 1970, during a very turbulent time in our society, the campus radical Megaphone Mark in a *DOONESBURY* cartoon was shown falling off to sleep. Above his head you could see this thought: "It's Christmas Eve as a tired, disappointed and disillusioned student activist drops off to sleep."

The next frame shows him sleeping. The frame after shows him stirring as if startled by an unexplained noise. In the final frame he explains, "I thought I heard reindeer."

Kirk Kirkpatrick: "Anyone who thinks Christmas doesn't last all year just doesn't have a Mastercard."

In the comic *FOR BETTER OR WORSE*, Elizabeth is singing a song which her mother is sure was taught to her by her father:

"Later on, we'll perspire,
As we stare at the fire,
An' face so afraid,
The bills left unpaid,
Walking in a winter wonderland."

❄ ❄ ❄ ❄ ❄ ❄ ❄ ❄ ❄ ❄ ❄ ❄ ❄ ❄ ❄

Dear Santa,

I've been such a good girl this year, networking like crazy in kindergarten. My lemonade stand had the highest after-tax profit in town. My brother, Justin, has been super, too. He was the first kid on our block to restructure the debt of his Little League franchise. So we just know that you'll get us everything on this list. We've made it easy for you. All our requests come from the 1987 F.A.O. Schwartz catalog....

First, I want the cute little ranch mink coat (p. 5, $2500). I'd also like the carousel music box (p. 4, $12,000). So what if it's gold plated?

Justin wants the Ferrari Testarossa Junior (p. 1, $14,500) so he can zip through the playground at 28 mph. Also, he'd like the 'Birthday Party of a Lifetime' (p. 5, $18,000). His friends will love staying at the Plaza and taking the horse-drawn carriage ride through Central Park. I told him the party might be just one of those things that grown-up catalog writers promise, maybe for publicity, and never expect to deliver.

But Santa, you're only three once.

Jennifer

P.S. This isn't like a bribe or anything, but there'll be Godiva chocolates waiting by the fireplace and some crudités for the reindeer. ❤ *Newsweek, 11/2/87, p. 73, 'For Kids Who Have It All: Minks and Cars'*

❄ ❄ ❄ ❄ ❄ ❄ ❄ ❄ ❄ ❄ ❄ ❄ ❄ ❄ ❄

In the comic, *CATHY* is stuck in a traffic jam trying to go do her normal shopping. As frustration seeps in and her car is unable to move, she says, "If stores really understood the holiday spirit, they'd open an express lane for the greedy."

In the cartoon, *SALLY FORTH*, Sally says to her mother after she has just viewed the large family Christmas tree with all the packages lying under it: "Have you ever noticed how one particular emotion gets real strong at Christmas?" Her mother answers: "I sure have, honey. I get very nostalgic at this time of the year. I especially like to think back to Christmas times when I was your age. My mind fills with memories of decorating the tree...singing carols...baking cookies...It's a big part of the holidays for me. I'm impressed that someone your age would recognize that nostalgia is such a strong emotion at Christmas time."

Sally goes back to the tree, looks at the huge pile of wrapped gifts and thinks to herself: "Nostalgia? I was talking about *GREED.*"

I read recently about a woman who had waited until the last minute to send Christmas cards. She rushed into a store and bought a package of 50 cards without really looking at them. Still in a big hurry, she addressed 49 of the 50 and signed them without reading the message inside. On Christmas Day, when things had quieted down somewhat she chanced to run upon the leftover card and finally read the message she had sent to 49 of her friends. Much to her dismay, it read like this: "This card is just to say/ A little gift is on the way." Suddenly she realized that 49 of her friends were expecting a gift from her--a gift that would never come.

I heard of a church that had a live outdoor Nativity Scene. For several nights prior to Christmas, members of the church would stand out there, dressed as members of the Holy Family or wise men or shepherds, freezing their ears off, trying to look properly reverent. They even had a live sheep. He was quartered in the parsonage garage, next door to the church. They didn't have a donkey, but I read recently of a church that did. They also had an outdoor Nativity Tableau. It was quite an undertaking, inasmuch as the church was located in the very heart of downtown in a large metropolitan area, and sheep and donkeys were hard to come by. But somehow they found one of each. The evening of the tableau everybody was busy making preparations. The donkey that was to be used in the pageant wandered off and trotted down the street. He caused quite a commotion, as you can imagine. Finally, he entered a nearby bar. Obviously, one of the customers was startled when he saw a donkey come into a bar. The customer pushed his glass aside and decided he had had enough. The bartender, seeing that he was startled, tried to calm him by saying, "Oh, don't let the donkey bother you. He belongs to the Methodist Church up the street." Thinking about that, the man decided it was time to leave.

A young family was going home for Christmas. The car was all packed. The mail and the newspaper delivery had been stopped. A neighbor would keep an eye on the house and feed the dog. All the gifts for parents, grandparents, aunts and uncles were somehow fitted into the trunk of the car. They had plenty of anti-freeze in the radiator. Their suitcases and hanging clothes were in place. They were finally ready to go. The husband started out of the driveway, when all of a sudden the wife gasped, "Honey, we've forgotten the baby."

Sometimes things get so hectic at this special time of the year that we are prone to forget the baby...

Santa Claus and an elf were having an argument. Santa said there were 49 states, and the elf said there were 50. Finally the elf went through Santa's list of states and found the one that was missing. With a big smile, he said to Santa, "Yes, Santa Claus, there is a Virginia!"

Someone has stated that the three phrases that best sum up the Christmas season are: "Peace on Earth," "Good will to men," and "Batteries not included."

One of our Jewish comedians tells about a Jewish lady named Mrs. Rosenberg who many years ago was stranded late one night at a fashionable resort on Cape Cod--one that did not admit Jews. The desk clerk looked down at his book and said, "Sorry, no room. The hotel is full." The Jewish lady said, "But your sign says that you have vacancies." The desk clerk stammered and then said curtly, "You know that we do not admit Jews. Now if you will try the other side of town..."

Mrs. Rosenberg stiffened noticeably and said, "I'll have you know I converted to your religion."

The desk clerk said, "Oh, yeah, let me give you a little test. How was Jesus born?"

Mrs. Rosenberg replied, "He was born to a virgin named Mary in a little town called Bethlehem."

"Very good," replied the hotel clerk. "Tell me more."

Mrs. Rosenberg replied, "He was born in a manger."

"That's right," said the hotel clerk. "And why was he born in a manger?"

Mrs. Rosenberg said loudly, "Because a jerk like you in the hotel wouldn't give a Jewish lady a room for the night!"

I read of a family out in Texas which had the custom of putting large plywood letters bordered with Christmas tree lights on their roof each year. The letters spelled out the word *"NOEL."* But one year the father, who usually did the job, had been especially busy. It was almost mid-December, and he had not yet put up the word *"NOEL."* The family had been after him to get it done, for the letters were big and clumsy, and only he could manage them. So he decided one Saturday that he would get it done that day, regardless. Well, that day was very windy, and the struggle was great. He fought the West Texas wind and muttered some rather un-Christmasy comments under his breath as he wrestled the gigantic plywood letters up onto the roof. It was nearly dark

when he finished, and he clambered down the ladder triumphantly to tell the kids to plug in the lights. They did. And the letters blazed forth against the darkening sky--*"LEONI"*
➥ From an Advent "Calendar of Devotions" by Jo Carr and Donna Cash, Abingdon Press, 1980, p. 29.

One woman to another as they looked at a manger scene and stained glass windows in a downtown store window in windy Chicago, "Humph, look at that, will ya. The church is trying to horn in on Christmas!"

Children's letters to Santa: "Dear Santa, My folks are getting the toys; you just bring the batteries...Matt."

A little boy in a Christmas program had but one sentence to say, "Behold, I bring you good tidings." After the rehearsal he asked his mother what "tidings" meant. She told him tidings meant "news." When the program was performed, he was so scared before the large congregation that he forgot his line. Finally the idea came back to him and he blurted out, "Hey, I got good news for you!"

Years ago a mother wanted to do something special to emphasize the meaning of Christ's coming into the world, so she purchased a beautiful candelabra, placed it prominently in the living room, mounted tall white candles on it, carefully lit each one and then called her six-year-old son into the room and asked him what this meant. He thought for a minute and answered, "Liberace's coming to dinner."

A group of first graders got together and decided to write their own version of the Nativity. It was more modern than the traditional drama. Oh, there were the familiar members of the cast: Joseph, the shepherds, the three wise men, the star and an angel propped up in the background. But Mary was nowhere to be seen. Suddenly from behind some bales of hay could be heard some soft moans and groans. Evidently Mary was in labor.

Soon a doctor arrived dressed in a white coat with a stethoscope around his neck. Joseph, with a look of relief on his face takes the doctor straight to Mary, then starts pacing back and forth. After a few moments the "doctor" emerges with a big smile on his face.

"Congratulations, Joseph," he says, "It's a God!"

There was a little book from Doubleday titled, *DEAR GOD, CHILDREN'S LETTERS TO GOD.* One young man wrote:

"Dear God, was there anything special about Bethlehem or did you just figure that that was as good a place as any to start a franchise?

Your friend, Jim age 12."

The newspaper sometimes run a famous *DENNIS THE MENACE* cartoon from years ago. It's Christmas afternoon and Dennis has finally gotten all of his presents opened. He is up to his chin in wall-to-wall toys. You can't see the floor for all his presents and gifts. The caption is a lament. Dennis says, "Is this all? Is this all I got this year?"

We may be like one young man I heard about whose grandmother sent him a shirt for Christmas. The only trouble was that he had a size 14 neck and the shirt was size 12. When the grandson sent a thank you note, he wrote, "Dear Grandma, thanks a lot for the shirt. I'd write more, but I'm all choked up."

CHURCH

Someone once compared his church to Noah's Ark. "If the flood on the outside were not so bad, you couldn't stand the smell on the inside."

Somewhere I read a true story about a chairman of a certain church committee who stood one Sunday morning before the congregation to present a minor matter of church business for a vote. After the vote, his next agenda item was to lead the congregation in singing several hymns. He confidently presented his project for a vote, fully expecting routine acceptance by the congregation. But to his surprise, the matter failed to win congregational approval. He was so completely rattled by this surprising turn of events that in introducing the next hymn, instead of inviting the group to join him in singing "I Stand All Amazed," he introduced it as "I Stand All Opposed."

Willard Scott, the irrepressible weatherman on the TODAY program on television wrote a book entitled *THE JOY OF LIVING*. A very appealing part of that book is his warm description of growing up in a Baptist church. He tells how on one occasion when he was twelve years old, he took communion and had a most embarrassing thing happen to him. He describes it like this:

"In the Baptist church, they serve grape juice rather than wine, in tiny little individual-sized plastic cups.

"On this particular occasion, I was trying to get the last bit of juice out of the bottom of the cup with my tongue, when all of a sudden the suction grabbed hold and my tongue got stuck in the cup!

"I tried desperately to pull that doggone cup off, but after the first couple of tries, it wouldn't budge. Then before I could make another attempt, the pastor asked everyone in the church to hold hands with the person next to him and sing 'Blest Be the Tie That Binds.' But I was the one in a bind. Here I was with this cup on my tongue, and the people next to me had grabbed my hands.

"But just when it seemed like I was about to be discovered, I had what I can only regard as a divine inspiration. I sucked the whole cup into my mouth and held it there until the hymn was over. Then, while no one was looking, I reached in and pulled it off my tongue." ∞ Willard Scott, *The Joy of Living,* (New York: Ballantine Books, 1982).

One man I heard about was asked why he quit singing in the choir. He answered, "I was absent one Sunday and someone asked if the organ had been fixed."

There is a cartoon showing a mother, a father, and a small boy leaving church. The father was wearing a look of annoyance and saying to his son, "I want you to stop referring to the church as the repentagon."

A man went to see his doctor for advice about his snoring. The doctor asked, "Does your snoring disturb your wife?" The patient replied, "Does it disturb my wife? Why it disturbs the entire congregation!"

John Ruskin defined a sermon as "thirty minutes in which to raise the dead."

Henry Ward Beecher once said: "If anyone falls asleep in church, I have given the ushers permission to wake up the preacher!"

Dr. Eugene Brice tells a disturbing story about a minister who returned to visit a church he had once served. He ran into Bill, who had been an elder and leader in the church, but who wasn't around anymore. The pastor asked, "Bill, what happened? You used to be there every time the doors opened." "Well, Pastor," said Bill, "a difference of opinion arose in the church. Some of us couldn't accept the final decision and we established a church of our own." "Is that where you worship now?" asked the pastor. "No," answered Bill, "we found that there, too, the people were not faithful and a small group of us began meeting in a rented hall at night." "Has that proven satisfactory?" asked the minister. "No, I can't say that it has," Bill responded. "Satan was active even in that fellowship, so my wife and I withdrew and began to worship on Sunday at home by ourselves." "Then at last you've found inner peace?" asked the pastor. "No, I'm afraid we haven't," said Bill. "Even my wife began to develop ideas I was not comfortable with, so now she worships in the northeast corner of the living room and I am in the southwest..."

☞ *Books that Bring Life* (Lubbock, Texas: Net Press, 1984)

There is a story of a young minister appointed to his first rural parish. He attended the county fair with the folks of the parish. And he was told that his predecessor had usually entered the hog-calling contest, and won. He was asked if he'd like to give it a try. He replied, "Well, when the Lord and the Bishop appointed me to serve this church, I thought I was being called to be the shepherd of the sheep...but you know your people better than I do!"

The story is told of a mother who called up the stairs to her son: "Get up! It is time to go to church." The son said, "Aw, Mom, I don't want to go to church. The people there all make fun of me. They don't really like me. Nobody there ever listens to what I say. I'd rather stay home in bed." The mother said, "But son, you've got to go." The son said, "Give me two good reasons." The mother replied, "Well for one thing, you are forty-two years old; and, for another, you're the minister!"

A pastor in a drought-stricken part of the South implored his people to begin praying for rain. In fact, he asked each member of the church to join in a prayer vigil that would continue day and night until God granted their request. Never had there been a greater sense of urgency in that church than was revealed over the next few days. At any hour, one might pass that small rural church and find the lights on and someone at the altar praying. Finally, late Wednesday evening, some dark clouds began to roll in. Soon rain began falling in torrents. For four straight days it rained without ceasing. The creeks began oveflowing their banks. It became necessary to evacuate persons from their homes. Still the water kept rising. The entire community was now under water. As rescue workers made their way in a boat through the perilous floodwater evacuating the last reluctant stragglers, one of the boats passed that little country church, now almost completely submerged. There sat the pastor on the roof of the church with a look of grand satisfaction on his face. He could be heard saying to himself as he surveyed the flood waters around him, "Not bad for a small church like ours. Not bad."

A teenager came home from choir practice early one evening. His father was incredulous. The boy had never come home early from anything. Looking over his paper he asked, "What brings you back so soon?"

"We had to call off choir practice for this week," the youth replied. "The organist and the choir director got in a terrible argument about how to sing 'Love Divine,' so we quit for tonight."

A group of women were talking together. One said, "Our congregation is sometimes down to 30 or 40 on a Sunday."

Another said, "That's nothing. Sometimes our congregation is down to 6 or 7."

A maiden lady in her 70s added her bit, "Why, it's so bad in our church on Sundays that when the minister says 'Dearly beloved,' it makes me blush."

Over the great front doors of a church being restored was the sign, *THIS IS THE GATE OF HEAVEN.* Just below it, a small sign read, *USE OTHER ENTRANCE.*

The pastor of a certain church was called to minister at another church. "The same God who sent me to you," the pastor announced, "is now calling me away."

There was a moment's silence, and then the congregation rose and began to sing, "What a Friend We Have in Jesus."

An elderly lady was being conducted through a tour of St. Peter's Bascilica, one of the great cathedrals of Europe. The guide spoke of the beauty of the design, calling special attention to its statues and wonderful masterpieces of art and painting. The lady was very unimpressed. At the conclusion of the tour, she asked the tour guide, "How many people have been saved here this year?" "My dear lady," said the embarrassed guide, "this is a cathedral, not a church."

Dear Folks,

Last Sunday we had a lot of folks absent from the church because of sickness and other reasons. But we prayed for the sick ones at home and I want to share with you what I saw when I rode around town Sunday afternoon...I saw Hazekiah who had been deathly sick that very morning, had roused up and was riding down the highway with his fishing poles. A miracle! Then there was Roberta's brother-in-law. She had requested prayer for him that morning because he might have to have an operation on his back. Well, prayer works because at two o'clock I saw him at the driving range hitting golf balls...But what made me really happy was to see so many shut-ins out riding and enjoying the world. Fran's Pa, who can't stand crowds (and don't attend church for that reason, was headed for the jockey lot. Tony's Mom, who was too weak to get out of the house, was uptown window shopping. Omega's older sister, who can't come to church on account of her kidneys, stood in line two hours to get into the picture show. Yep, it really thrilled my heart to see what I saw. I ought to have a packed house next Sunday with all my folks being healed and shut-ins set free. I just hope they don't overdo themselves next Sunday and have a relapse.

Yours for more miracles,
Parson Jones. ∽ Contributed by Wade Burton

I came across an interesting "confession" recently by George Knight, "Football Games Are Not For Me," which has appeared in many bulletins:

"I've made up my mind never to attend another football game. I've been an avid fan for many years, but now I've had it. Let me list my reasons:

1. My parents took me to too many games when I was growing up.

2. The games are always played when I want to do something else.

3. Every time I go to a game, someone asks for money.

4. Although I attend the games frequently, few of the other poeple are friendly or speak to me.

5. The seats are too hard and uncomfortable. Besides, I often have to sit down front on the fifty-yard line.

6. I suspect there are hypocrites in the crowd.

7. The field judge says things I don't agree with.

8. The band usually plays some numbers I don't especially like--some I've never even heard before.

9. Some games last too long, making me get home late

10. I've got a good book on football. I can stay at home and read that."

There have been many innovative ideas set forth to aid the church in becoming what it was intended to become. There have been creative programs offered, special designs in buildings to enhance our worship and study, and many more. Perhaps one of the most innovative architectural designs is found in a legend from New England.

The pastor of the church had bemoaned the fact that no one seemed to feel involved in worship service. The people could not be motivated to go into the world properly because they held back so much in worship. He found an architect who promised to build a badly needed worship center if the church would agree to keep the plans secret until it's unveiling on the day it was first to be used. They agreed (it must not have been a Baptist church).

The big day finally arrived. The building looked very normal from the outside. The big difference was on the inside. A great crowd gathered early that first Sunday. Each person was seated on a pew near the door, one pew at a time. When the pew was filled, it was rolled automatically to the front! This process continued until the entire sanctuary was filled. The preacher was so carried away by having his audience at the front, he didn't really get warmed up until twelve o'clock! In the middle of one of his most fervent appeals, at two minutes past twelve, a trap door opened, and the preacher dropped into the basement! ∽ Don Emmitte

A group of clergy were discussing the raising of Lazarus in the Gospel of John, chapter 11.

One pastor, looking puzzled, broke in: "Why did Jesus ask the people to push away the stone, when He could perform miracles?"

Another pastor hastily replied, "Involvement of the laity, of course!"

The preacher in *KUDZU* is standing beside one of those outdoor "banking machines" set in front of a new church with a sign which reads: "24-Hour Donations!"

Robert Schuller tells a ridiculous story about two men sitting on a river bank. The night was still except the sound of a chorus of crickets. One of the men commented, "Crickets sure do sing." The other answered, "Yep, they sure do." As he was saying this he heard the sounds of a choir rehearsing at a nearby church. "Sure is beautiful music, isn't it?" he said. The first man, lost in thought, replied, "And to think they do it by rubbing their legs together."

There is a corny story about a little girl in a mountain family who laid her head over on her father's ample midriff in a worship service and went to sleep. The mother, seeing her daughter cushion her head in this fashion, whispered to her husband, "There, Clyde, now you know what it means to be a pillar o' the church."

You probably know the story about the little boy who went to church with his grandparents. His grandmother sat in the choir. It really disturbed her to see grandfather nod off to sleep every Sunday in the middle of the sermon. Finally, she decided on a plan. She gave her little grandson fifty cents each Sunday morning to poke grandpa in the ribs whenever he fell asleep. This plan worked until Easter Sunday morning. The church was packed. Grandmother was sitting in the choir. She noticed grandfather nodding off. However, Tommy made no effort to wake him. Grandfather even started snoring right there in the crowded Easter service. Still Tommy did nothing. After the service grandmother was quite disturbed. She said, "Tommy, what happened? You knew I would pay you fifty cents after the service if you kept grandfather awake." Tommy said, "Yes Ma'am, but grandfather offered me a $1.00 if I would let him sleep."

There's another little story concerning two boys who were talking about Noah and the ark. They were thinking about the odors and the noise and the inconvenience of being cooped up on the boat with all of those animals--about how crowded and about how dirty, and about the problem of separating animals that were natural enemies and so on. One of the boys said, "I just don't think I could stand that." And the other little boy thought for awhile and he said, "Well, yes, it must have been awful. But think of it the other way. It was still the best thing afloat."

That's the way I feel about the church. It ain't perfect, but it's still the best thing afloat...

A cartoon in *THE CHURCHMAN* magazine sometime back showed a small boy standing before a very large church door, and asking the minister in the doorway, "Is God home?"

A "typo" in a church bulletin: "The ushers will eat all the latecomers."

One overcommitted Christian went to see his pastor one day about his runaway wife. "And when did she leave you?" the minister asked. "I'm not sure," said the layman. "It was sometime between Monday and Friday of this week. I've been at church every night, and I can't honestly say when it was."

The minister glared down at Joe Smith and roared, "And are you, my son, a soldier in the army of the Lord?"
Surprised at being singled out, Smith replied anxiously, "Y-yes sir, I am."
"Then why," pressed the clergyman, "do we see you here only at Christmas."
Thinking quickly, Smith replied, "Would you believe, sir, I'm in the secret service?"

A Sunday School teacher challenged her children to take some time on Sunday afternoon to write a letter to God. They were to bring back their letter the following Sunday. One little boy wrote, "Dear God, We had a good time at church today. Wish You could have been there."

Paul Conn in his book, *MAKING IT HAPPEN*, tells how one day while living in Atlanta he noticed in the Yellow Pages, in the listing for restaurants, an entry for a place called The Church of God Grill. Curious, he dialed the number. A cheery voice answered, "Hello! Church of God Grill!" Conn asked the man on the other end how his restaurant had been given such an unusual name. Here was the man's answer:

"Well, we had a little mission down here, and we started selling chicken dinners after church on Sunday to help pay the bills. Well, people liked the chicken, and we did such a good business, that eventually we cut back on the church services. After a while we just closed down the church altogether and kept on serving the chicken dinners. We kept the name we started with, and that's Church of God Grill."

An associate pastor in Sturgis many years ago, tells a delightful story that happened during one Christmas Eve service: "Near the end of the service, the Senior Pastor whispered to me, 'I think we are going to run out of elements. You count the cups, I'll count the congregation.' I did. He said: 'There are 33 people left to commune, how many communion cups do you have? I said, '16.' He said, 'Get some more grape juice.' I said, 'Where?' He said, 'That's your problem.' I tried to excuse myself unobtrusively, and went to the church kitchen where the attendants had carefully prepared the cups and bread cubes. It was closed down tight. What to do? Then I remembered that I had a half-empty bottle of grape juice left from a communion which I had a couple of months previously. What had I done with it? Oh, yes, I put it in (of all places) my filing cabinet. (Probably filed under "J" for juice, instead of "W" for wine.) Sure enough, there it was. But the cap was stuck on tight. How to open it? I reached into my pocket and extracted a pair of fingernail clippers. With that device I succeeded in prying off the cap. Poof! It popped off, grazing my cheek, leaving a visible scar, and smoke poured out of the neck of the bottle. I then poured the stuff into some little cups (ignoring the instructions in the hymnal which say, "The pure, unfermented juice of the grape shall be used." In an emergency, you have to go with what you've got!) I hurried back into the sanctuary. The pastor looked quizzically at me, as though I had just performed the miracle of the loaves and the fishes. And, as it turned out, the choir got the old juice, and they seem to have survived. On the way up the aisle, the pastor whispered, 'Where did you get the juice?' 'I'll tell you later,' I said. After the service, when I told him what happened, he doubled up with laughter. I said, a Scripture verse occurs to me. 'What is it?' 'You have saved the best wine until the last!' (John 2:10) And so it goes. ⌀Dr. Donald Strobe

COMMITMENT

The conductor of the community orchestra was almost out of his mind. At every single rehearsal, there had been at least one member who had been missing. Planning for a well organized concert was almost impossible.

At the last rehearsal, he called for attention and said, "I would like to thank the first violinist for being the only member of the orchestra to attend every rehearsal."

The violinist smiled shyly and humbly said to the conductor, "Well, it seemed the least I could do since I won't be at the concert tonight."

COMMUNCATION

I like Zig Ziglar's story of the woman who went to her pastor for counseling concerning her marriage. After a few preliminaries, the pastor said he had a few questions that would help identify the problems if she would just answer as openly as possible. When the lady agreed, he began by saying, "Do you have any GROUNDS?" To which the lady responded, "Why, yes we do, we have about ten acres just north of town." "No, ma'am," the pastor replied, "that's not what I mean. What I mean is do you have....well, do you have a GRUDGE?" "Oh, no," she replied, "but we do have a nice little carport!" "No, ma'am," said the pastor, "that's not what I meant. One more question: Does your husband beat you up?" "Beat me up? Oh, no, I get up before he does just about every morning!" In complete exasperation the pastor said, "Lady, you're not listening to me. Why are you having trouble with your husband?" "Well," she said, "the man just doesn't know how to communicate!"

Zeke and May had been married for over seventy years. The man was one hundred and one years old. His wife was ninety-nine. One hot afternoon they sat on the front porch rocking. The old man was nearly deaf. The wife looked over at him with admiration in her eyes and said, "Zeke, I'm proud of you." He looked around and said, "What's that you say, May?" She raised her voice, "I'm proud of you!" He looked away. "I'm tired of you, too, May," he said.

John R. Claypool tells a delightful story that he picked up in Texas about a certain Mexican bank robber by the name of Jorge Rodriguez, who operated along the Texas border around the turn of the century. He was so successful in his forays that the Texas Rangers put a whole extra posse along the Rio Grande to try and stop him. Sure enough, late one afternoon, one of these special Rangers saw Jorge stealthily slipping across the river, and trailed him at a discreet distance as he returned to his home village. He watched as Jorge mingled with the people in the square around the town well and then went into his favorite cantina to relax. The Ranger slipped in and managed to get the drop on Jorge. With a pistol to the thief's head he said, "I know who you are, Jorge Rodriguez, and I have come to get back all the money that you have stolen from the banks in Texas. Unless you give it to me, I am going to blow your brains out." There was one fatal difficulty, however. Jorge did not speak English and the Texas Ranger was not versed in Spanish. There they were, two adults at an utter verbal impasse.

But about that time an enterprising little Mexican came up and said, "I am bilingual. Do you want me to act as translator?" The Ranger nodded, and he proceeded to put the words of the Ranger into terms that Jorge could understand. Nervously, Jorge answered back: "Tell the big Texas Ranger that I have not spent a cent of the money. If he will go to the town well, face north and count down five stones, he will find a loose one there. Pull it out and all the money is behind there. Please tell him quickly." The little translator got a solemn look on his face and said to the Ranger in perfect

English, "Jorge Rodriguez is a brave man. He says he is ready to die."

I heard about one poor man who had a very difficult mother, but he felt obligated to take care of her. He had a basement apartment built in his home just for her. One day a friend of his paid a visit. They were chatting in the living room. "I remember," said his friend, "what a difficult time your mother gave you. Where is the old girl now?" Fearing that the conversation would be overheard, the poor man simply pointed downward in the direction of the basement apartment. "Oh, I'm sorry," said his friend, "I didn't even know she had died."

NEWSWEEK recently cited a humorous historical footnote that reveals how easily communications can be garbled. Some of you can remember the moving speech that President John F. Kennedy gave at the Berlin Wall in 1963 which he ended by saying, "Ich bin ein Berliner." Literally that translates to "I am a Berliner," but according to NEWSWEEK, in the German vernacular it really translates as "I am a jelly doughnut."

An article in the PRAIRIE OVERCOMER sometime back revealed that a few years ago gifts to the Prairie Bible Institute of Alberta, Canada, declined from a certain geographical area. At that time the school's president, Dr. Maxwell, had undergone two operations for cataracts, one for each eye. A representative of the school was visiting in the area where the giving had declined, when one of the regular supporters of the school asked him, "What's this about President Maxwell driving around in two Cadillacs?" That was the rumor that had spread. Cataracts had become Cadillacs and people were witholding their support.

Tom Stoppard has one of the characters in the play "Night and Day" saying: "I'm with you on the free press. It's the newspapers I can't stand."

There is an old story about a woman who was vacationing in Florida where she discovered a very valuable piece of art that was being sold. She sent her husband a telegram describing the work and informing him of the price. Her husband wired her back immediately, whereupon she went directly to the gallery and purchased the piece of art. Taking it home with her, she was greeted by her husband who was irate. "I wired you direct instructions," he said, "that you were not to purchase that work." She was flabbergasted. "I have your wire right here," she said. "Read it for youself." He did and learned how important punctuation is, for the telegram read, "No price too high." He had intended to say, "No! Price too high."

I read recently about a born loser. I doubt that the story is true. However, strange things do happen in life.

A young man knocked on the door of an expensive home seeking odd jobs to earn money. The owner suggested he should paint the porch using the green paint in the garage. A few hours later, the young man, covered with green paint nearly from head to toe, returned to get his pay. As he pocketed the $50.00, he said, "By the way, sir, that's not a Porsche--it's a Ferrari!"

In some cultures people communicate as much, or more, with gestures as with words. An old Jewish peddler ambled down a street in Tel Aviv carrying two large watermelons. A tourist stopped him to ask, "Where is Ben Yehunda Street?" The peddler answered, "Please hold these two watermelons." The tourist managed to gather them in his arms, whereupon the peddler made an expansive gesture with his hands and exclaimed petulantly, "How should I know?"

One problem in communication is that some people just don't get the joke. A caterer was instructed by a man posing as a cat food manufacturer to prepare a banquet for four prize cats. The concerned caterer asked about the sex of the cats.

When queried as to why that was important, he noted, "Well, it would be so nice to have an alternating seating arrangement of a male and female cat." The caterer put together a menu starting with lobster bisque and designed a centerpiece of celery for the cats to play with. After being told that he was actually being filmed for CANDID CAMERA, and after he had given his permission to broadcast the segment and was about to leave, he turned and said in all seriousness, "About that banquet--I'll need at least four weeks' notice." Ꮿ Alan Funt in *Laughing Matters*

COMPASSION

Somebody has facetiously developed a flyer called *THE AMERICAN FOSTER PARENT PLAN.* The brochure reads like this: "Poor nations! Adopt an American! For only $26,000 per year you can adopt an American child and provide the basic necessities of life: television, roller skates, and twinkies.

"For years you Third World countries have subsidized American gluttony. Now you can be specific and choose your individual American child and know him by name." Then we are shown a cartoon of a cute little over-fed American child on roller skates with a caption reading like this: "Little Brad above is nine years old. He has a cheap stereo and only one good leisure suit and is forced to live in a tri-level. There are many others like him. Write today!" Ꮿ Tom Sine, *Why Settle for More and Miss the Best?* (Waco: Word Books, 1987), pp. 169-70.

A man walked into the post office one day and purchased a card. He turned to the man next to him and requested, "Sir, would you mind addressing this card for me?" The man, thinking the poor fellow could not write, gladly helped him out. When he handed the card back, the man needed another favor. "I hate to bother you again," he continued, "but would you mind writing a short message on the card for me?" The kind gentleman agreed to this second request and wrote out the message as the man dictated it to him. He gave the completed card to the man who looked at it for a moment and then asked one more favor. "I know this is an imposition, but would you mind doing one more thing for me? At the end of the message, would you apologize for the horrible handwriting?"

A guy is lying face down on a busy street. Traffic is backed up for blocks. A little old lady rushes up and begins giving him artificial respiration--whereupon he swivels his head and says: "Look lady, I don't know what game you're playing, but I'm trying to fix this cable beneath the street."

Some years ago the readers of Charles Schultz's *PEANUTS* comic strip saw Snoopy shivering out in a snow storm beside an empty fooddish. He was looking longingly, expectantly, toward the house. Lucy came out and said, "Go in peace, be warmed and filled!" And then she turned and went back into the house and slammed the door. In the last frame you saw a confused Snoopy looking toward the house, shivering and hungry and utterly baffled.

COMPETITION

Some people will do anything to win. The early days of baseball provide many notable examples. Before stadiums had permanent seats in the outfield, for example, teams were permitted to erect temporary bleachers or simply put up a rope if a large crowd was expected, and any ball hit into that area was ruled a ground-rule double. When Ty Cobb was managing the Tigers and a power-hitting team was visiting, he would have the ground-crew set up temporary bleachers, turning balls that might otherwise have been home runs into ground-rule doubles. And if the crowd wasn't large enough to justify putting up the seats, Cobb would have the ground-crew sit in those bleachers so the umpire would not order them removed. In Chicago, Cubs' fans standing behind the outfield rope would push forward toward the infield when the home team was at bat, thereby shortening the field, and then back up several steps when the visitors came to bat, thereby causing some would-be homers to fall short.

When Bill Veeck owned the Cleveland Indians, he moved the outfield fences in or out depending on the lineup of the visiting team. When the league finally passed a rule prohibiting that, Veeck compensated: He would go out to the ball park at night, dig up home plate, and move it a few feet forward or backward. ∞ Ron Luciano and David Fisher, *Remembrance of Swings Past*, New York: Bantam Books, 1988).

As a nation our chief competitor continues to be the Japanese. There is a story going around that had George Bush in a coma for three years. He woke to find Dan Quayle standing at his bedside. Upon seeing the Vice President, the President begins to ask a few questions.

After asking questions we might expect about his health and his family he inquires about the state of the U.S. economy. To his surprise, Quayle tells him that the budget and trade deficits have been reduced to zero. Then, President Bush asks about inflation. Again, to his surprise, Quayle says that inflation is not a problem. Having his doubts, the President asks for specifics. "How much," he asks "does a first class stamp cost?" "Very reasonable," Quayle responds. "Only 30 Yen."

The trouble with the rat race is that even if you win, you're still a rat. ∞Lily Tomlin

COMPLIMENT

I am reminded of a young couple who were sitting out on porch swing. She asked, "George, do you think my eyes re beautiful?" George answered, "Yep." In a few moments: George, do you think my hair is attractive?" Again George nswered, "Yep." In a while: "George, would you say that I ave a gorgeous figure?" Once again George answered, Yep." "Oh, George," she said, "You say the nicest things."

CONVERSION

There was a fellow in the South who wasn't very deep in is commitment to Christ but who loved to go to Revival meet- gs. Every time a visiting evangelist put up a tent on the out- kirts of town, he was there. When the invitation was given at he close of the service this man would be the first one to the ltar. Kneeling at the altar he would spread out his arms and ray loud enough for everyone in the service to hear, "Fill me, ord Jesus, fill me."

Every revival that came to town, he would follow this ame ritual. He would be the first one to the altar and he would ray, "Fill me, Lord Jesus, fill me." Finally, a lady who knew im well couldn't take it any longer. Once when he was pray- g that same empty prayer, "Fill me, Lord Jesus, fill me," she tood up and prayed loudly, "Don't do it, Lord. He leaks!"

William P. Barker tells about a machinist with the Ford notor company in Detroit who had, over a period of years, borrowed" various parts and tools from the company which e had not bothered to return. While this practice was not con- oned, it was more or less accepted by management, and othing was done about it. The machinist, however, ex- erienced a Christian conversion. He was baptized and became a devout believer. Even more importantly, he took his baptism seriously.

The very next morning he arrived at work loaded down with tools and all the parts he had "taken" from the company during the years. He explained the situation to his foreman and added that he'd never really meant to steal them and hoped he'd be forgiven.

The foreman was so astonished and impressed by his action, that he cabled Mr. Ford himself, who was visiting a European plant, and explained the entire event in detail. Immediately Ford cabled back: "Dam up the Detroit River," he said, "and baptize the entire city!"

I heard about a very somber minister all dressed in black many years ago who was driving in his buggy along a lonely country road when he overtook a young man walking along that same road. The minister stopped and with dark, gloomy tones invited the young man to ride with him. As they were riding along, the minister thought to himself that he had not said anything to this young man about his soul. So in a deep ministerial voice he asked, "Young man, are you prepared to die?" With a face as white as death the young man jumped over the back of the buggy and lighted on the ground. Rushing down the road he shouted back, "Not if I can help it!"

I am reminded of the story of a man who was walking alone in a deserted area of the country. Suddenly he tripped and fell into a deep well. From way down in this well he yelled for help as loudly as he could, but nobody could hear him. Finally exhausted, the man realized he was going to die. So he prayed frantically, "Dear God, please get me out of this."

All of a sudden there was an earthquake, and the man was shot to the surface. He was profoundly grateful. A few months later, the same man was walking through that deserted area again with a friend. When they came to the well, he suddenly shoved his friend into it, so he could have the same experience of deliverance that he had.

Many of us are like the first-grader who was in a Sunday School class that was quizzed by the pastor on the meaning of certain religious words like "baptized," "repentance," etc. The little boy was asked, "What is conversion?" He thought for a moment and gave the only definition that he knew. "It's the extra point that is kicked after a touchdown," he said.

COURAGE

One fellow noted that the national sport in Spain is bull fighting while in England it is Cricket. He decided to go to England. Fighting crickets, he decided, is much easier than fighting bulls.

One comedien was recovering from a head-on crash. It wasn't his fault, he said. The highway sign said, "Do not cross center line if yellow." He had to show them he wasn't.

A rich woman from New York was touring the West and finally arrived in Santa Fe. She noticed an old Indian with a necklace made from curious-looking teeth. "What are those?" she asked.

"Those are grizzly bear teeth, madam," replied the Indian.

"Ah, yes," she nodded. "And I suppose they have the same value for you red men that pearls have for us."

"Not exactly, madam," replied the noble savage. "Anybody can open an oyster."

"Is it true," a reporter asked a safari guide, "that jungle animals won't harm you if you carry a torch?" -- "That depends," replied the guide, "on how fast you carry it."

There is a humorous story about Bob Zuppke, the colorful football coach at the University of Illinois. Zuppke was trying to get his team prepared to play the University of Iowa. "Men," he roared, "I want you to get in there and die for Illinois. Nobody will be taken out unless he's dead. Get that? Unless he's *DEAD!*"

The inspired but overmatched Illinois played Iowa to a standstill until late in the fourth quarter when they finally ran out of gas. In fact, one of the frail Illinois halfbacks literally keeled over from exhaustion. Zup grabbed one of his younger players and yelled, "Get in there and replace that man!"

The youth dashed out to where the exhausted man lay --then came right back to the sidelines. "What's wrong?" shouted Zuppke. "Why didn't you take that man's place like I told you?"

"It ain't necessary, Coach," gulped the youngster. "He's still breathing a little."

I like the story of the little boy, a first grader, who strutted up in front of his classmates and proclaimed, "When I grow up, I'm going to be a lion tamer. I'll have lots of fierce lions, and I'll walk in the cage and they'll roar." He paused a moment, looking at his classmates' faces, and then added, "Of course, I'll have my mother with me."

Two small boys walked into the dentist's office. One of them said, "I want a tooth taken out and I don't want any gas, and I don't want it deadened because we're in a hurry!"

The dentist said, "You're quite a brave young man. Which tooth is it?"

The boy turned to his smaller friend and said, "Show him your tooth, Tommy."

COURTESY

An amusing story came out of the Coolidge administration. An overnight guest in the White House wanted to make a good impression. He was having breakfast with President

Coolidge. He noticed with some discomfort that the President, having been served his coffee, took the coffee cup, poured the greater portion of its contents into a deep saucer, and leisurely added a little bit of sugar and a little cream. The guest felt that since the President had followed this procedure, so should he. So he also poured out much of his coffee into his saucer and added sugar and cream. Then he watched with dismay as the President took his saucer and put it on the floor for the cat. We are not told what the guest did next.

CREATION

PONTIUS' PUDDLE cartoon: Pontius is looking out over the world and says, "Wow! A carpet of lush grass dotted with turquoise lakes lined by emerald trees set against a lavender mountain range--all showcased under an azure sky!
"God makes a great exterior decorator!"

The late Dr. E.J. Daniels, refuting evolution: "I might have had some ancestors who hung by their necks from a tree, but not a single one ever hung from a tree by their tail."
∽ Wade Burton

A boy in biology class said, "It would not make any difference to me if my grandfather had been a monkey."
A brighter lad beside him said, "It sure would have made a difference to your grandmother."

A second grader once asked his teacher how much the earth weighed. The teacher looked up the answer in an Encyclopedia. "Six thousand million, million tons," she answered. The little boy thought for a minute and then asked, "Is that with or without people?"

In the cartoon, *ZIGGY* contemplates the world around him. He looks at the sunrise and says, "Gosh!"

He looks at the flowers and bees and thinks, "Beautiful!" He watches the clouds go by, looks at the mountains and the fish jumping in the lake, and finally the sunset. He takes a deep breath and says, "Actually, God stays pretty busy on His day off!"

CREATIVITY

It was a beautiful summer day and Clarence was enjoying a row in the boat with his lovely girlfriend, anticipating the picnic they would have when they got to the island in the center of the lake. These were days when young men and young ladies wore more than shorts and t-shirts when out in public. Clarence had donned a spiffy suit with a high collar, and his female companion had on a long dress with billowing petticoats underneath. Clarence masculinely pulled on the wooden oars as his date sat coolly under her parasol. Though the steamy heat of the summer day began to wring sweat from him, he was so hypnotized by his girlfriend's beauty he was not troubled. Finally he reached their location, dragged the boat onto the shore and helped his girlfriend out of the boat.

He placed all their supplies beneath a spreading shade tree, and as he prepared to sit down and enjoy the coolness of the shade, the girl said gently, "Honey, you forgot the ice cream."

"Ice cream?" stammered Clarence, recalling that the two had planned an ice cream dessert. So the suitor got back into the boat and stroked his way back across the lake. He found a grocery store, bought some ice cream, and headed back for the cool shade where his date sat.

Upon arriving at the island once more, his girlfriend had another friendly reminder: "Clarence, honey, you forgot the chocolate syrup."

Clarence was in love. So he got back into the boat,

grabbed the hot oars once more, and set sail for the grocery store on the shore. He bought the syrup, returned to the boat, and once again began rowing in the hot afternoon sun. But this time the frustration of it all got to him, and half way to the other side, he put up the oars and began to think. There must be a better way.

By the end of the afternoon, Clarence Evinrude had invented the outboard motor. The girl he left stranded on the island became his wife, and the company he started used the above story in it's first ads for the revolutionary new outboard motor. ∽ Lewis Timberlake in *TIMBERLAKE MONTHLY*

CRITICISM

Lucy screams: "You Stupid Beagle! You Fat, No-Good, Worthless Hound!"

Snoopy slinks away thinking to himself: "That's the trouble with being sensitive...even the slightest remark can hurt your feelings."

William Muehl of Yale Divinity School tells of visiting a fine old ancestral house in Virginia. The aged owner was the last of a distinguished colonial family, and she was proudly showing him through the home. Over the fireplace he noticed an ancient rifle which intrigued him. He asked if he might take it down and examine it. She replied, "Oh, I am afraid that wouldn't be safe. You see, it is all loaded and primed to fire. My great-grandfather kept it there in constant readiness against the moment when he might strike a blow for the freedom of the colonies." Prof. Muehl said, "Then he died before the Revolution came?" "No," she answered, "he lived to a ripe old age and died in 1802, but he never had confidence in George Washington. You see, he knew him as a boy and didn't believe he could ever lead an army!"

An outstanding Prime Minister of Australia was once the victim of a vicious verbal attack in Parliament by a member of his own party. When the traitor had finished speaking, the Prime Minister rose to his feet and cupped his hand to his ear, as if listening for something. Knowing the Prime Minister to be rather deaf, one of his colleagues asked what he was waiting for. "I'm waiting for the cock to crow," he replied.

J.G. Morrison tells us that John Wesley, the founder of the Methodist church, was riding along a road one day when it dawned on him that three whole days had passed in which he had suffered no persecution. Not a brick or an egg had been thrown at him for three days. Alarmed, he stopped his horse, and exclaimed, "Can it be that I have sinned, and am backslidden?"

Slipping from his horse, Wesley went down on his knees and began interceding with God to show him where, if any, there had been a fault.

A rough fellow, on the other side of the hedge, hearing the prayer, looked across and recognized the preacher. "I'll fix that Methodist preacher," he said, picking up a brick and tossing it over at him. It missed its mark, and fell harmlessly beside John. Whereupon Wesley leaped to his feet, joyfully exclaiming, "Thank God, it's all right. I still have His presence."

A retired man tells how he always used to go to Bill Meyer Stadium in Knoxville, Tennessee, to watch the Knoxville Smokies play baseball. He says that there was an old man at the stadium who never missed a game. He would sit in the same seat each game and invariably offered the same chant. Whenever a Knoxville Smokey came up to bat he would yell, "Walk him, pitcher, walk him." If the pitcher should walk the batter, then the old man would yell triumphantly, "You walked the wrong man, pitcher, you walked the wrong man."

I have always felt sorry for football coaches. They have to put up with an amazing amount of grumbling from alumni, sporstswriters and even the average man in the street. I like what former Wake Forest football coach Chuck Mills once said. He defined a spectator as a person "who sits forty rows up in the stands and wonders why a 17-year-old kid can't hit another 17-year-old kid with a football from forty yards away...and then (that same spectator) goes out to the parking lot and can't find his car."

DEATH

Woody Allen once said that he was not afraid of dying. He just didn't want to be there when it happened.

George Burns in his book, *HOW TO LIVE TO BE 100-- OR MORE*, has a chapter entitled, "Stay Away from Funerals, Especially Yours." George says that if you look in the obituary column in the morning and your name isn't there,"go ahead and have breakfast."He says that if he ever looks in the obituary column and finds that his name is there, he will still have breakfast. "I'm not leaving on an empty stomach," he says.

There is an old story about a court jester who was once given a wand by the nobleman he served. "Keep this," said the nobleman, until you find a greater fool than yourself." The jester put away the wand and kept it for many years. One day the nobleman lay dying. Calling the jester to his side, he said, "I am going on a long journey." The jester asked, "Where to?" The nobleman shrugged his shoulders. "For how long?" asked the jester. "Forever," replied the nobleman weakly. "What provisions have you made for your journey?" asked the jester. "None," answered the nobleman. "Then," said the jester, "take this," and he handed the nobleman his wand. "For you are a greater fool than I."

We are kind of strange in our attitude toward death. Dr. Joe Harding tells about a funeral home in Florida that guaranteed to get you to heaven.

"They advertised a dramatic innovation in burial services. For about $4,000 they would cremate your body, put it into a small rocket, and fire it into orbit! It was guaranteed to circle the earth for 2,300 years! Perhaps, one of the selling points of the new idea would be that on a clear night people could come out, look up at the heavens and watch you go by. I am sure that someone will even put identifying blinking lights on the satellites so that people can say, 'There goes George! There is Mary! There is Bill! They are all up there with their friends.'"

I enjoy the story of a man named Fred Abernathy who was a devoted reader of the obituary column of his local paper. All of Fred's friends knew of this habit, so one day they decided to play a trick on him by placing his name and picture in the obituaries.

The following morning Fred picked up his newspaper, turned to the obituary page, and there he saw his name, his biography and his photo.

Startled, he went to the telephone and rang up his pal, George. "Listen," he said. "Do you have the morning paper? You do? Please turn to the obituary page. You have? What do you see in the second column?"

There was a pause, then George said, "Holy smoke! It's you, Fred! It's you all right! Listen, where are you calling from?"

As Woody Allen said, "It is impossible to experience one's own death objectively and still carry a tune."

As George Bernard Shaw once remarked, "Life's ultimate statistic is the same for all men: one out of one dies."

Before George Burns became a star in his own right, he was better known as the straight man for his delightful wife, Gracie Allen. They worked together for many years in radio and television. After her death he visited her grave regularly. An interviewer jokingly asked him if, on these visits to her grave, he told her what had been going on. "Sure, why not?" was the reply. "I don't know whether she hears me, but I've nothing to lose and it gives me a chance to break in new material."

At the death of Nikita Kruschev many years ago, a humorous story circulated in political circles. The Communist party that had cast Mr. Kruschev aside was uncomfortable with the idea of burying his body on Soviet soil. They first called the President of the United States, Richard Nixon, and asked if the U.S. would take Kruschev's corpse. Nixon had his own problems at the time and declined. Then the Soviet leaders tried Golda Meir, Prime Minister of Israel. Mrs. Meir was agreeable but she added, "I must warn you that this country has the world's highest resurrection rate."

Soon after the 1929 crash, a cemetery in Pennsylvania was forced to put up a sign: *PERSONS ARE PROHIBITED FROM PICKING FLOWERS FROM ANY BUT THEIR OWN GRAVES.*

*D*ECISION

"Next year I'm going to be a changed person!" Charlie Brown tells Lucy.

"That's a laugh, Charlie Brown!" she says.

"I mean it!" he replies. "I'm going to be strong and firm!"

"Forget it," she says as she walks off. "You'll always be wishy-washy!"

"Why can't I change just a little bit?" Charlie Brown asks himself. "I'll be wishy one day," he shouts, "and washy the next!"

Bernard Tristain once won a newspaper competition by providing the best answer to this question: "If a fire broke out in the Louvre and you could save only one painting, which one would it be?" His reply was, "The one nearest the exit."

"Mr. President," a reporter asked Truman, "are you afraid of making mistakes?"

"No," Truman said. "If I were, I could never make a decision. I have to make a decision every day, and I know that fifty percent of them will be wrong. But then that leaves me fifty percent right, and that's batting five hundred."

"How do you handle the fifty percent wrong?" the reporter asked.

Truman replied, "I laugh at them, and at myself, and so does Bess."

A mother took her three children into the ice cream parlor for an ice cream cone. The man behind the counter asked, "Chocolate or vanilla?" The mother asked, "Why don't you have more flavors?" "Lady," he answered, "if you only knew how much time it takes some people to make up their minds betweeen chocolate and vanilla, you'd never have another flavor!"

I believe it was Yogi Berra who once said, "When you come to a fork in the road, take it!"

Teddy Roosevelt had a little dog that was always getting into fights and always getting licked. Somebody said, "Colonel, he's not much of a fighter."

The colonel replied, "Oh, yes, he's a good fighter. He's just a poor judge of dogs."

Some people get lost in thought because it's unfamiliar territory to them.

Those of you who are sports fans will appreciate the story of a college football team whose starting quarterback was injured. The number two quarterback had not even dressed out due to illness. This left only a freshman quarterback who also did their punting but had absolutely no game experience as a college quarterback. The coach had to throw him into the fray anyway. It was first down, but the ball was resting on their own three yard line. The coach's main thought was to get them away from the goal line so they would have room to punt out of danger.

The coach said, "Son, I want you to hand-off to Jones, our big fullback for the next two plays, let him run into the middle of the line and get us a few yards. Then I want you to punt." The young quarterback did as he was instructed. On the first play he handed off to Jones, but almost miraculously Jones found a hole off tackle and ran fifty yards. The young quarterback called the same play again and once more, miracle of miracles, the hole was there again. This time Jones ran forty five yards. The fans were going crazy. The ball was on the opponent's two yard line--six short feet of the goal line.

Confidently, the team lined up quickly and the young quarterback received the snap, stepped back and punted the football into the stands. As the team came off the field, the coach angrily grabbed the young quarterback and asked, "What in the world were you thinking about when you called that last play?" The quarterback answered blankly, "I was thinking what a dumb coach we have."

A Sunday school teacher was telling the story of the rich man and Lazarus. There sat Lazarus outside the rich man's gate covered with sores and begging for food. Passing by without even seeing Lazarus was the rich man. But then they both died and Lazarus went to Heaven, while the rich man found himself in less desirable circumstances, which the teacher described most graphically.

When she had finished, she asked the children, "Now which would you rather be--the rich man or Lazarus?" One little fellow answered, "I would like to be the rich man until I die and then Lazarus afterwards."

EDUCATION

Parents of college students get poorer by degrees.

Someday we are forced to face the facts of life for ourselves, as the head of a college of business administration pointed out when he called all the students together upon the completion of the course. He spoke to the graduates as follows: "Now that you have finished your course, I want to tell you one more thing. Half of all you have been taught here is wrong. But the trouble is, I don't know which half."

A girl at Bennington named Louise
Weighed down with Ph.D's and D.D.'s
Collapsed from the strain.
Said her doctor, "It's plain
You are killing yourself -- by degrees."   ∞ *Anon.*

There is a lot of concern about education nowadays. Jaime O'Neill is a college teacher in Washington. He decided to give his students a basic facts test; not trick questions, mind you, but a simple test to illustrate to his students that they needed to get serious about learning. Here's what he found from a survey of college students:

"Ralph Nader is a baseball player. Charles Darwin invented gravity. Christ was born in the 16th century. J. Edgar Hoover was a 19th-century president. The Great Gatsby was a magician in the 1930's. Franz Joseph Haydn was a songwriter who lived during the same decade. Sid Caesar was an early Roman emperor. Mark Twain invented the cotton gin... Jefferson Davis played guitar for the Jefferson

Airplane. Benito Mussolini was a Russian leader of the 18th century; Dwight D. Eisenhower came earlier, serving as a president during the 17th century...Socrates (was an) American Indian chieftan...."

The professor goes on, "My students were equally creative in their understanding of geography. They knew, for instance, that Managua is the capital of Vietnam, that Cape Town is in the United States, and that Beirut is in Germany...Camp David is in Israel, and Stratford-on-Avon is in Grenada. Gdansk is in Ireland...Belfast was variously located in Egypt, Germany, Belgium and Italy. Leningrad was transported to Jamaica; Montreal to Spain."

Someone saw this sign on a college bulletin board: "Books for sale -- like new. Hardly used."

Many schools are in crisis. I like what comedian Joe Hickman said: "At first I wanted to be a cop, but you have to be 6'1", know karate, and carry a gun. Then I thought I'd be a schoolteacher, but you have to be 6'1", know karate, and carry a gun." ∞ *Quote*

A first-grade teacher summed up herself as "a person whose job is to welcome a lot of live wires and see that they are well grounded."

The high school debater stepped confidently to the podium, spread out a raft of notes, cleared her throat and prepared to present the affirmative of the topic: "Modern Education Doesn't Meet the Needs of the Day."

As she stared intently at her notes, however, bewilderment spread over her face. "I'm sorry," she finally stammered, "I've got it all written down here, but darned if I can read it."

"Sit down, young lady," offered an elderly member of the audience. "You've won the debate."

EGO

A ridiculous story has been making the rounds lately. It is about a pilot and three passengers--a boy scout, a priest, and an atomic scientist--and a plane that develops engine trouble in mid-flight. The pilot rushes back to the passenger compartment and exclaims, "The plane is going down! We only have three parachutes, and there are four of us! I have a family waiting for me at home. I must survive!" With that, he grabs one of the parachutes and jumps out of the plane.

The atomic scientist jumps to his feet at this point and declares, "I am the smartest man in the world. It would be a great tragedy if my life was snuffed out!" With that, he also grabs a parachute and exits the plane.

With an alarmed look on his face, the priest says to the boy scout, "My son, I have no family. I am ready to meet my Maker. You are still young with much ahead of you. You take the last parachute."

At this point, the boy scout interrupts the priest: "Hold on, Father. Don't say any more. We're all right. The world's smartest man just jumped out of the plane wearing my knap sack!"

As someone has said, "The person patting you on the back may only be determining where to stick the knife."

Teddy Roosevelt was such an outgoing person with a bombastic personality that the story circulates that on Teddy Roosevelt's first day in heaven he said to St. Peter, "Your choir is weak, inexcusably weak! You need to reorganize it at once." St. Peter assigned Roosevelt the task of reorganization. Roosevelt immediately responded, "I need ten thousand sopranos, ten thousand altos, and ten thousand tenors." St. Peter inquired, "But what about the basses?" "Oh," said Teddy, "I'll sing bass!"

Elizabeth Barrett, meeting Wordsworth for the first time, wrote ironically, "He was very kind to me and let me hear his conversation."

Vice President Quayle, who has taken a lot of kidding since being nominated for and elected Vice President, says he's getting help in "keeping the pomp and glitter in perspective." He and his family and the Secret Service dined at Red, Hot & Blue--an "in" ribs place in Washington, D.C. When Quayle stood to leave, applause broke out. Quayle said he was pleased--until the headwaiter told him people in line were clapping because his party had just vacated three tables.
➣ *USA TODAY*, 1/31/89, p. 4A.

Many years ago this bit of gossip was printed in a London newspaper about a famous painter and an equally famous writer: "James McNeil Whistler and Oscar Wilde were seen yesterday at Brighton talking, as usual, about themselves."

When Whistler saw that little tidbit of gossip in the newspaper, he clipped it out and sent it to Oscar Wilde with a note that said, "I wish these reporters would be more accurate. If you remember, Oscar, we were talking about me."

Oscar Wilde replied in a telegram that said, "It is true, Jimmy, that we were talking about you, but I was thinking of myself."

In her biography of Winston Churchill, Kay Halle tells the story of a little boy who lived near Chartwell and was taken there by his nanny to see "the greatest man in the whole, wide world." Churchill had retired for his afternoon nap. While the little boy's nanny had her tea, the child sneaked off to look for his hero and found him reading in bed. "Are you the greatest man in the whole wide world?" the boy asked. To which Churchill replied, in good Churchillian fashion: "Of course I'm the greatest man in the whole wide world. Now buzz off."

One of Teddy Roosevelt's sons once said of him, "Father always wants to be the bride at every wedding and the corpse at every funeral."

Paul Harvey told recently about a college basketball coach who was shaving when his wife called upstairs to tell him that SPORTS ILLUSTRATED was on the phone. The coach was so excited he nicked himself shaving. Hewas so eager for recognition for himself and his school that rushing to the phone he fell down the stairs and bruised himself up. Staggering to the phone breathlessly, he said, "Hello." The voice at the other end said, "Yes, sir. I'm happy to tell you that for only 75 cents per week you can receive a one year's subscription..."

One of the amazing things in our society is to see people who delight in trampling all over others in order to satisy their own selfish whims. Someone sent us an absurd story about a customer who went into a bakery shop, the finest, most expensive in New York. There he ordered a very elaborate cake to be prepared in the shape of an "M". He insisted that on a specific date it must be ready.

The day before the deadline the insistent customer arrived to see how the cake was progressing. "Oh, this is all wrong," he yelled. "You've made a capital 'M' cake. I wanted a lower-case 'm'. I will be by here the same time tommorrow and I expect my cake to be done right."

The manager apologized profusely, and assured the man that his cake would be finished by tomorrow and would be done right.

The customer returned the next day to find his cake decorated to his every whim. "That is fine," he said. "Just as I wanted it."

"Now, sir," said the proprietor, "where would you like it sent?"

"Don't bother," said the customer. "I'll eat it here."

A little boy was told to come directly home from school, but he arrived late almost every day. His mother asked him, "You get out of school the same time every day. Why can't you get home at the same time?" He said, "It depends on the cars." "What do cars have to do with it?" asked his mother. The youngster explained, "The patrol boy who takes us across the street makes us wait until some cars come along so he can stop them."

EXPERIENCE

Do you know the story of the two hunters who flew deep into remote Canada in search of elk? When they started back home, their pilot, seeing that they had bagged six elk, told them the plane could carry only four out. The hunters protested. "The plane that carried us out last year was exactly like this one. The horsepower was the same, the weather was similar, and we had six elk then." Hearing this, the pilot reluctantly agreed to try. They loaded up and took off. Unfortunately, the plane did not have sufficient power to climb out of the valley with all that weight, so they crashed. As they stumbled from the wreckage, one hunter asked the other if he knew where they were. "Well, I'm not sure," replied the second hunter, "but I think we are about two miles from where we crashed last year."

EXPERT

A well-known Yale geology professor, when asked by a student the age of a fossil, replied with considerable authority that it was two million and three years old. Incredulous over his ability to so precisely date such an old object, students asked how the professor knew with such certainty. He explained that another group had visited the same site three years earlier and had been told by a local farmer that the fossil was then two million years old.

FAILURE

In a *PEANUTS* cartoon Charlie Brown is complaining that his ball team always loses. Lucy tries to console him by saying, "Remember, Charlie Brown, you learn more from your defeats than you do from your victories."

Charlie Brown replies, "That makes me the smartest man in the world."

Some years ago *TIME* magazine reported on a nervous motorist in Lambertville, New Jersey. This man, on being stopped by the police, explained that he had been driving on two hundred and twenty-four consecutive learner's permits over the last twenty-five years. He had flunked his first driver's test and had been unsure of himself ever since! ✆ George F. Regas, *Kiss Yourself and Hug the World* (Waco: Word Books, 1987).

FAHNESTOCK'S RULES FOR FAILURE: If at first you don't succeed, destroy all evidence that you tried.
✆ *Murphy's Law, Book 2.*

Recently I heard about a football coach in one of our Southern football factories, who was experiencing the horrors of a losing season. By the middle of October the Alumni were in a state of near mutiny. The first week in November, after a particularly embarrassing loss to a traditional arch-rival, the coach received a telegram which read as follows: "The last train out of town leaves Sunday at noon. Be under it!"

As that plaintive philosopher Snoopy once said in a *PEANUTS* cartoon, "It doesn't make any difference whether you win or lose--until you lose."

*F*AITH

One of the most told stories of the past decade has to be the story of a man named Henry who lived in a valley near a river. The river had reached flood stage. Everybody was being evacuated to higher ground. Except Henry. He was staying at his house and not abandoning it. God would take care of him, he contended. Soon the water had risen to Henry's porch. His friends paddled by in a rowboat. Henry was sitting on his windowsill. "We have come to save you, Henry," they said. Henry would not budge. "God will save me," he said. It was not long before the flood waters had risen several feet. Henry was now stranded on the second floor. A rescue team came by in a motorboat. As he waved to the people from the window, they shouted to him, "Henry, we've come to ave you." Henry said, "Don't worry about me. God will save me." Finally, Henry was sitting on top of his roof. A helicopter hovered overhead and someone shouted through a megaphone, "Henry, grab the rope before it's too late." But Henry would not budge. The waters rose higher. Henry drowned.

As Henry entered the gates of heaven the Lord met him. "Lord," said Henry, "I'm glad to meet you, but frankly, I am very disappointed. I counted on you to save me, but you let me drown." "Henry," said the Lord, shaking his head and smiling with understanding, "I sent a row boat, a motor boat, and even a helicopter to save you. What more did you want me to do?"

A certain preacher was preaching mightily about the need to trust the Lord. "The good Lord is going to take care of us," he said. As he lifted his arms, however, his coat parted and the congregation noticed a pistol tucked into his pants. After the service, one of his members said, "Preacher, I thought you told us we could trust the Lord." "Yes, brother," he said, "you sure can." The member retorted, "Then why are you carrying that pistol around?" Without missing a beat, the pastor said, "That's to hold the enemy off until the Lord gets here."

A man, wishing to embarrass the local pastor, rose and suddenly called out quite loudly, "There is no God."

The pastor went to him, calmly laid his hand on his shoulder, and said, "Friend, what you have said is not at all new. The Bible said that more than 2,000 years ago."

The astonished man replied, "I never knew that the Bible made such a statement."

The pastor replied, "Psalm 53, verse 1, tells us, 'The fool says in his heart, there is no God.' But there is one great difference between that fool and you. He was quite modest and said it only in his heart; he didn't go about yelling it out for all the world to hear."

My friend and former parishioner, Hall of Fame quarterback Bart Starr, made me the pleasant butt of a joke in a service club speech several years ago with this story: "Dr. Kalas was playing golf recently with a Catholic friend, Father Joseph Schultz. On each of the first three holes when they got to the green, Father Schultz made the sign of the cross and then sank a long and almost impossible putt.

"After watching this scenario three times Dr. Kalas asked, 'Joe, do you think it would help my putting if I make the sign of the cross before approaching the ball?'

"'No,' Father Schultz answered. But Dr. Kalas wasn't about to just take no for an answer, so he asked, 'Why not? Because I'm a Protestant?'

"'No,' Father Schultz replied, 'because you don't know how to putt.'" ↪ J. Ellsworth Kalas, *The Power of Believing*, (Waco, Texas: Word Books, 1987).

Chuck Swindoll tells a true story about a kindergarten teacher who was determining how much religious training her new students had. While talking with one little boy, to whom the story of Jesus was obviously brand new, she began relating his death on the cross. When asked what a cross was, she picked up some sticks, and fashioning a crude one, she explained that Jesus was actually nailed to that cross, and then he died. The little boy, with eyes downcast, quietly acknowledged, "Oh, that's too bad." In the very next breath, however, the teacher related that Christ rose again and that He came back to life. And the young boy's little eyes got as big as saucers. He lit up and exclaimed, "Totally awesome!"

One of the great truths of the Christian faith is that salvation is free--it need not be earned. This simple truth is so often misunderstood even by devout Christians. They remind me of a story that is told concerning the madcap pitcher of the St. Louis Cardinals, Dizzy Dean:

In the 1930's America was still primarily a rural nation, and Dizzy was the archetypal small-town farmboy who came to the big leagues with a blazing fastball and enchanted fans with his homespun humor. Dizzy had an ego so large that by comparison Muhammad Ali was shy, but he also had the talent to back up his boasts. Certainly part of Dean's original appeal was his naivete. When he first joined the Cardinals' "Gashouse Gang" in 1930, for example, he rode up to the hotel's seventh floor in the elevator with roommate Rip Collins. It was probably the first time Dean had ever stayed in a hotel. Collins asked the bellboy to bring some ice, and tipped him when he delivered it. Dean asked Rip why he had paid the bellboy. "That was for the elevator ride," Collins explained. "They didn't charge me," Dizzy pointed out.

"They know you're with the team," Collins said, "so they just put it on your bill." For the next three days Dizzy climbed the stairs to get to his room. ∾ Ron Luciano and David Fisher. *Remembrance of Swings Past*, (New York: Bantam Books, 1988).

FAMILY

A lecturer singled out an individual from the audience and asked if he would be willing to walk across a narrow steel beam hypothetically resting on the floor in exchange for $20 if he succeeded. Answering affirmatively, the question was then changed to one of the same beam suspended between two forty-story buildings with the result that the student-executive promptly indicated he would not undertake the walk under such circumstances and certainly not for $20. Having seemingly made his point, the lecturer inadvisedly continued, posing still another question: "Supposing I were standing on one of the same two buildings holding one of your children over the edge and told you I would drop your kid if you didn't walk across the beam. *NOW* what would you do?" Pondering momentarily, the executive made a shambles of the decorum of the class when he inquired, "Which kid do you have?"

On a trip to Texas, we stopped in New Orleans and visited the zoo in Audobon Park. My wife and I were walking ahead of my sister and her husband. As we neared a pen where there was a gray-haired chimp, we noticed some boys were yelling at him. They'd go to the water fountain, get a good mouthfull, and spit water at the chimp. We saw the chimp go to his water bowl and sip water. The next time the boys neared the cage, he spat water on them! Then he went back to the water bowl and returned to his perch. The boys had left. But along came my brother-in-law. I resisted telling him about the spitting chimp. And when he got close to the cage, SPEEEW! The chimp splattered him good. ☞ Wade Burton

After graduating from college and landing my first job, I moved into a small apartment. As I was proudly showing my parents my new home, I noticed that my father was going into each room and needlessly turning on all the lights. Puzzled, I asked him why.

Dad grinned happily. "I've waited twenty-two years to be able to come to your house and leave the lights on!" he replied. ❧ Scott Fienne in *Reader's Digest*

I was reading a humorous account about a young couple who were trying to decide what kind of child birth method to use. Like most couples having children nowadays, they were investigating the benefits and shortcomings of natural childbirth. A friend had a warning for the wife, however. "There's one major flaw in that program," she said. "No one told me that having the baby was going to *HURT*."

There's an amusing story about a descendant of the famous brothers, William and Henry James. This young man grew up in Cambridge, Massachusetts, and got thoroughly sick of everybody saying every time he was introduced, "Oh, James--any relation to Henry and William?" He went out to Colorado, where people said, "Oh, James--any relation to Frank and Jesse?" He stayed in Colorado.

The story is told of a rabbi at one of the larger yeshivas who was famed for his orderly thinking processes and facile wit. One day, during philosophy class, a grinning student asked, "Rabbi, would you rather have five daughters or five thousand dollars?"

"Five daughters," answered the rabbi instantly.

"But that is based on emotion, not cold reason," protested the youth.

"My preference is based on pure logic," the rabbi said evenly. "First, human nature being what it is, if I had five thousand dollars I would undoubtedly want more. As a pious man I cannot condone greed, even in myself. You will agree that this cannot possibly apply to five daughters. Secondly, should I desire to have five thousand dollars it would not happen anyway; simple desire without practical application does not produce money. So why make a fool of myself? Thirdly, young man, I would rather have five daughters because I actually have eight!" ☞ *The Encyclopedia of Jewish Humor*

"Grandpa," she complained, "you have a horrible voice. Why do you insist on singing in the shower?"
"Because," said grandpa with sweet reason, "there's no lock on the bathroom door."

Occassionally we are like terrible-tempered Lucy in the *PEANUTS* comic strip. Lucy comes into the room where Linus is watching TV. He says to her, "I was here first, so I get to watch what I want." Without a word Lucy marches to the set and flips the channel to her program. Linus protests. "Hey!" Assuming her best know-it-all stance, Lucy intones, "In the 19th chapter of the book of Matthew it says, 'Many that are first will be last, and the last first.'" Linus's response to this paradox sounds like something you or I would say. He mutters, "I'll bet Matthew didn't have an older sister!"

During the Civil War, humorist Artemus Ward boasted, "I have already given two cousins to the war, and I stand ready to sacrifice my wife's brother."

Herbert Prochnow tells of a little girl who wrote in an essay on *PARENTS*: "We get our parents at so late an age that it is impossible to change their habits."

One day a little girl asked her mother, "Mommy, why does Daddy bring so much work home at night?" "Because he doesn't have time to finish it at work," answered the mother. "Then why don't they put him in a slower group?", asked the little girl. ☞ *Laughing Matters*

The story is told of a young boy who wanted a new suit of clothes, and he asked his mother if she would ask his father to buy it for him. The mother suggested that it might be better if the boy would ask the father himself. The response of the boy was, "Well, I would, but you know him much better than I do."

A Sunday School teacher was teaching the importance of love in the home. She illustrated her point by referring to the commandment, "Honor thy father and thy mother." Then she asked if there was a commandment which taught how to treat sisters and brothers. One little boy from a large family raised his hand quickly. Innocently he asked, "Thou shalt not kill?"

A little girl had done something wrong and her mother told her to go to the corner and said very harshly to her, "You will sit there until your father gets home." The little girl stuck out her lip and said, "I'll stand in the corner but I won't sit in the corner." Her mother went to where she was standing, took her shoulders and forcibly sat her down. When the father came home he asked the little girl what she was doing sitting in the corner. She said defiantly, "My head tells me I'm sitting in the corner. But my heart tells me I'm still standing."

A grandmother was bidding a granddaughter good-night one evening when the child remarked, "Mommy and Daddy are entertaining some very important people downstairs." The grandmother agreed, "You're right. How did you know they were important?" The little girl said, "Just listen. Mommy is laughing at all of Daddy's jokes."

A grandmother got a note from her son and daughter-in-law that her grandchildren would be coming to spend a week with her. She loved her precious little granddaughter and lively little grandson, and when she thought about the pleasures that awaited her with them in her home, she went to church and put five dollars in the offering plate as a token of thanksgiving. She kept her grandaughter and grandson for that week and what a week it was. When they went home, she went back to church and put in a twenty dollar bill in the offering plate in thanksgiving.

"I'm really worried," said one teenager to another. "Dad slaves away at his job so I'll never want for anything and so I can go to college. Mom spends every day washing and ironing and cleaning up after me, and she takes care of me when I'm sick."

"So what are you worried about?"

"I'm afraid they might try to escape!" ⌒Jack Moore, Universal Press Syndicate

Two ladies were discussing their families. "Do you mean to tell me that your son and daughter-in-law were married six months ago and you haven't visited them yet?" exclaimed the first lady. "I'm shocked!"

"What's to be shocked?" demanded the second lady. "I'm waiting until they have their first baby. Everybody knows that a grandma is always more welcome than a mother-in-law."

ZIGGY by Tom Wilson points out the problems some of us face when Mother and Father are peering through their window into a snow laden landscape as they watch a car pull up to their house and Mother says, "We move over the river and through the woods and *STILL* they find us!"

It is not easy being a father. One cynic, speaking from his own experience, noted that children go through four fascinating stages. First they call you Da-Da. Then they call you Daddy. As they mature they call you Dad. Finally they call you collect.

One morning after church, a member asked her little son, "How was Sunday School?"

He answered, "Oh, all right."

The mother persisted, "Just all right? Who was your teacher?"

The little boy replied, "Well, I don't know but she must have been Jesus' grandmother. He was all she talked about."

FATHERS

The following discussion took place between my husband and our nine-year-old son:

"It's not fair, Dad. Mom wants me to make my bed, but I don't know how."

"It's time you learned. Where are your clean sheets?"

"I don't know."

"What do you mean you don't know? You need to keep track of your things."

"Where are Michael's sheets?" my husband called to me.

"Right next to ours," I replied.

After a prolonged silence, my husband asked sheepishly, "Where are ours?" ☞ Brenda Barton in *Reader's Digest*

A young fellow at college couldn't get home for Christmas. So he sent his Dad a set of inexpensive cuff links and a matching inexpensive tie clasp. Along with these gifts he sent a little note: "Dear Dad; This is not much, but it's all you could afford."

One little boy defined Father's Day like this: "Father's Day is just like Mother's Day, only you don't spend as much on a present."

Another child put it this way: "Mommy, if the stork is supposed to bring babies, if Santa Claus brings presents, if the Lord gives us our daily bread and Uncle Sam our Social Security, why do we keep Daddy around?"

One time, when Teddy Roosevelt was in the oval office discussing matters of state with a friend, his daughter Alice kept popping in and out, interrupting.

"Theodore," said his friend, "isn't there anything you can do to control Alice?"

Roosevelt replied firmly, "I can be President of the United States, or I can control Alice. I cannot possibly do both!"

Three little girls were trying to wake their father up one early Saturday morning. They giggled and yelled. They tickled his feet, poked his ribs, and pulled his ears, all with no result. One of them finally lifted up one of her father's eyelids.

"I don't know why he doesn't answer," the little girl said. "He is in there."

Several years ago a newspaper ran a contest for children on the subject "My Pop's Tops" just before Father's Day. Here are some of the entries:

"My pop's tops because he is not got a bad tempir. He dont get mad easy, but when he does he allus has a good reasin--me."

"...because he lets me help him work in the garden even if I don't want to."

"He lets me take acordine lessons and practice outside. When I practice outside he goes inside. He can tell better from a distance."

"He is never to tired to sit strawled in his easy chair telling stories while we children wash up the dishes."

"Every child should love their father because if it was not for their father where would they be? Nowhere, that's where they'd be. If it wasn't for fathers you wouldn't see hardly no children around Milwaukee." ∞ Anonymous in *The Clergy Journal*

America's favorite father, Bill Cosby, has an amusing routine in his book on fatherhood about the first parent. The first parent, according to Cosby, was not Adam or Eve. The first parent was God. Even God had trouble with his kids, according to Bill Cosby.

The first thing that God said to his kids was what most parents say to their kids, "Don't." And Adam replied, "Don't what?" And God said, "Don't eat the forbidden fruit." And Adam said, "Forbidden fruit? Really? Where is it?"

Bill Cosby says, "That's beginning to sound familiar isn't it? You never realized that the pattern of your life had been laid down in the garden of Eden."

"It's over there", said God, wondering why he hadn't stopped after making the elephants. A few minutes later God saw the kids having an apple break and He was angry. "Didn't I tell you not to eat that fruit?" the first parent said. "Uh-huh," Adam replied. "Then why did you?" God asked. "I don't know," Adam said. "Oh right, then, get out of here, go forth, become fruitful and multiply," said God. Cosby goes on to comment that this was not a blessing, but a curse. God's punishment was that Adam and Eve should have children of their own. Then he goes on to comment about the problems Adam and Eve had with their kids --one murders the other.

$\mathcal{F}$EAR

You can learn something from cartoons. For example, in a *DENNIS THE MENACE* cartoon, Dennis, a frightened little boy, had just climbed into bed between his mother and father. Dennis says, "I wouldn't be scared of the thunder if I could keep my mind off my thoughts."

Fear is relative. (I'm afraid of my brother-in-law. Just kidding.) A pretty performer stood quietly against a wooden background while her partner threw knives, hatchets, etc., into the wood around her as part of the vaudeville act. All at once, during the act, she screamed and fell over in a faint. The audience, of course, suspected the worst. But in her dressing room, when she had revived, she explained: "I suddenly felt something crawling on my leg and discovered a spider. Oh, I'm so afraid of spiders!"

Do you know why climbers making their way up steep, treacherous terrain tie themselves together with rope? One cynic said it is to keep the sensible ones from going home.

I like the story about the mountaineer who had been gone from home for over a week and when he came back home his clothes were torn, his shoes were worn thin, and it was obvious that he was exhausted. His wife put her hands on her hips and said with suspicion, "Where in tarnation have you been?"

"I went out in the woods to check the still," replied the mountain man, "and a giant bear stepped out in front of me. I took off running ahead of him and finally lost him. I never ran so fast in my life!"

"But that was a week ago," said the wife. "Where have you been since?"

"I've been walking back," he said.

FORGIVENESS

There is a story about two little boys who were fighting, as little boys are often prone to do. One of them yelled at the other, "I'll never speak to you again."

They went to their respective houses, but the next day they were back out playing as if nothing had happened. One of the little boys' mother asked him why they were speaking to each other now.

He responded, "Me and Johnny are good forgetters."

When our eldest son reached five, I decided to let him solo with his night prayers. He soon mastered the Our Father, Hail Mary, and Angel of God.

Then I let him try the Act of Contrition. Something sounded peculiar, so I leaned closer and asked him to start over. He closed his eyes and confessed, "Oh, my God, I am partly sorry...." I trust that the Lord has a good sense of humor ∞ Jack Walsh, *Catholic Digest*

*F*REEDOM

An American history teacher posed the following question to her class: "A distinguished foreigner was a big help to the American colonists during the Revolutionary War," she said. "Can anyone give me his name?" One young fellow felt he knew the answer. "It was God," he said.

There was a story in *QUOTE* magazine recently that tells it all. It seems that in Vienna, Austria, American, French, British and Russian soldiers share jeeps for military police duty. One group of them used to kill time by telling jokes. That is, the western soldiers did, for the Russians remained silent and sullen. The American asked, "What's the matter with you, Ivan? Doesn't anything funny ever happen in Russia?"

"Have you heard of the great canals in Russia?' Ivan asked.

"Yes," the American replied. "It must have been a hard job building them."

"Exactly," Ivan said. "They were built by people who told jokes."

A Russian wolfhound and a French poodle met on a Paris street. "How are things in Russia?" the poodle asked.

"Couldn't be better," the Russian wolfhound said. "I sleep in a solid gold doghouse on a carpet, and all day long they feed me caviar."

"If things are that great, why do you come to Paris?"

The Russian wolfhound looked around and whispered into the poodle's ear, "Sometimes I like to bark!"

Freedom isn't free. It cost mightily. A recent immigrant to America was describing to a friend his beautiful new print-- the famous patriotic work, "The Spirit of 1776." He said, "There are three men in it--one with a fife, one with a drum, and one with a headache."

There was a sweet lady who asked an English friend, "Do the English have the Fourth of July?"
With a perfectly straight face, he replied, "No madam, we go straight from the third to the fifth."

Jack Paar put it flippantly, but accurately, "Immigration is the sincerest form of flattery."

I was amused to read that an English lady accosted George Beverly Shea after a Billy Graham Crusade in London. She felt it was in poor taste for him to sing an American patriotic song as part of the crusade. He wondered what in the world she was talking about. She said she heard him sing, "It took America to put the stars in place..." Of course he sang, "It took a miracle..." but that is not what she heard.

The children in the first grade were singing "God Bless America." The teacher heard one little girl singing it this way: "Stand beside her, and guide her, with the light through the night from a bulb."

The students in a Junior High American history class were given an examination. Among the questions to be answered was the following: The Declaration of Independence was written chiefly by ... [fill in the blank.] On one of the papers, a student had written, "Candlelight."

Little kids are shown a model of the Statue of Liberty and are asked what she is doing. One child said, "She was taking a shower." Another said, "She was raising her hand because she knew the right answer, but she was cheating because she had a book of answers in the other hand."☞ *Candid Camera*

*F*RIENDS

Dennis J. DeHaan tells a great story about a farmer who was bothered by some crows that were pulling up his young corn. So he loaded his shotgun and crawled unseen along a fence row, determined to get a shot at the marauders. Now, the farmer had a very "sociable" parrot who made friends with everybody. Seeing the noisy offenders in the field, the bird flew over and joined them (just being sociable, of course). His owner saw the crows but didn't notice the family pet. He took careful aim, and--BANG! When he climbed over the fence to pick up the crows he had shot, he found his parrot--badly ruffled and with a broken wing, but still alive. He tenderly carried it home, where his children met him. They saw that their pet was injured, and they tearfully asked, "What happened to Polly, Father?" Before he could answer, the parrot spoke up. "Bad company! Bad company!"

A friend is somebody who doesn't go on a diet when you're fat. ☞ Erma Bombeck

*F*UTURE

"How I wish I could see what the stock market will be doing a year from now," an eager-beaver investor mused. "If I knew ahead of time what stocks would go up, I would buy heavily, and I would make a mint!"

He got his wish. Before him appeared a full newspaper page listing hundreds of stocks and their prices, dated one year ahead. But when he happened to flip the page, he saw the obituary column. His name was included.

There's an old story about a man who was nearly panic-stricken on his first flight. The pilot came back personally to calm him down. "Are you a religious man?" the pilot asked. "Yes," the man replied. "Don't you believe that when your time is up, you'll go and not until then?" the pilot asked. "Yes," the man replied. "Then what are you nervous about?" the pilot asked. The man said grimly, "I'm afraid your time will come before mine."

A misprint of the weather forecast read like this: "There is a five percent chance of today and tomorrow."

I got a chuckle reading about a man in New England in 1938. He went into an Abercrombie and Fitch store there and bought a new barometer. He took it home and proudly placed it on a window sill. He consulted it to see what the weather would be like that day. He couldn't believe it. The barometer said "hurricane." Here he was in New England. Hurricanes are for Florida. He grabbed that barometer and stalked back down to the Abercrombie and Fitch store to return it. The store clerk asked, "What's the matter?"

He said, "This barometer you sold me is defective. It's reading hurricane."

The store owner said, "Oh, we'll happily refund your money."

He got his money back and started home. By the time he got home, his house had been blown away by the hurricane that hit New England in 1938.

I love Al Jolson's great line, "Chances are we ain't seen nothin' yet!"

A mother was heading up the stairs with a basket containing the last load of folded clothes. She was also herding her three little ones in front of her for bedtime. Her eldest child, Peggy, who was then in kindergarten, picked that moment to begin one of those questions that seem to intrigue all children at some time. "Mommy," she asked, "If it were the end of the world, and everyone was getting ready to die..." The mother stopped, shifted the basket on her hip, and said an ultra-quick prayer for wisdom to answer this question. "Yes?" she prodded her daughter. The little girl finished her theological inquiry: "If the end of the world came, would you have to take your library books back?"

GIVING

One pastor told his congregation, "Your church is in real financial need. Quite frankly, it is fit to be tithed."

A pastor was laboring over his church's institution of a new unified budget. One budget would replace several smaller budgets. It took him a long time to determine the best way to present this. Finally he told the congregation that the new unified budget was their effort to "put all their begs into one ask it."

Do you remember that old, silly story of the minister who was exhorting his congregation to become more active in church affairs, to get the church on its feet? "Brothers and sisters," he proclaimed, "What this church needs is the energy to get up and walk." One of his deacons said, "Let her walk, brother, let her walk!" The preacher raised his voice a little and added, "But we can't be satisfied with walking, we've got to pick up speed and run." The deacon responded enthusiastically, "Run, yes, let her run!" The preacher was really getting into his message now. "But running's not enough either," he said. "One of these days this church has got to fly!" That same deacon echoed, "Let her fly! Let her fly!" The preacher paused for a moment and said solemnly, "But if this church is going to fly, we are all going to have to work harder and give more money!" The deacon said softly, "Let her walk, brother, let her walk."

One day a pastor was summoned to the home of an obviously poor man who was trying to live on $4,000 a year. The pastor talked with him for awhile and finally said, "Let's begin at the beginning and have a word of prayer in which we will dedicate one tenth of your income to the work of Christ." "No problem," thought the man, "that's only $400 a year and that isn't much nowadays. Why, that's only $8.00 per week." So they prayed together, and he promised to give back 10% to the Lord and the Lord's work. Over the years this man became quite wealthy, and eventually came to the point where he was making almost $100,000 a year! He came to the pastor and said: "I'd like to be released from that promise I made many years ago. One tenth of my income is now $10,000 a year, and I have some other plans for that." "No problem," said the pastor, and as they bowed in prayer the minister prayed not for the release of the promise, but that the man's salary would be reduced to $4,000 once more so that he could again afford to tithe. The man jumped up from the prayer and stamped out of the room muttering something about, "That isn't what I had in mind at all!"

The late Peter Marshall, chaplain of the Senate and Presbyterian pastor in Washington, had a prayer which ought to give us pause. He prayed, "Lord, help me to regulate my giving according to my income, Lest thou shouldst regulate my income according to my giving!"

There is an old story about a very wealthy man who died and went to heaven. An angel guided him on a tour of the celestial city. He came to a magnificent home. "Who lives there?" asked the wealthy man. "Oh," the angel answered, "on earth he was your gardener." The rich man got excited. If this was the way gardeners live, just think of the kind of mansion in which he would spend eternity. They came to an even more magnificent abode. "Who's is this?" asked the rich man almost overwhelmed. The angel answered, "She spent her life as a missionary." The rich man was really getting excited now. Finally they came to a tiny eight-by-eight shack with no window and only a piece of cloth for a door. It was the most modest home the rich man had ever seen. "This is your home," said the angel. The wealthy man was flabbergasted. "I don't understand. The other homes were so beatuiful. Why is my home so tiny?" The angel smiled sadly, "I'm sorry," he said. "We did all we could with what you sent us to work with."

David Rockefeller of Chase Manhattan Bank was traveling through South America. A group of bank officials of the government of Uruguay invited him for lunch. They were hoping for a sizable loan. The affair was held at a club that was famous locally for its buffet. Rockefeller passed through the line first. Thinking this to be the entire meal, he served himself generously. Once seated, he noticed that the others had taken skimpier portions. "I have so much," he said to the president of Banco Central, "and you have so little...." "I'm glad you mentioned that Mr. Rockefeller," interrupted his host, "because that's exactly what we want to talk to you about!"

One fellow said to another, "Say, I heard that you bought a new car. How did you ever afford it?"

The other fellow replied, "I just cancelled my church pledge."

The first one said, "Gee, I wish that I could buy a new car for that little."

There was a farmer who was interested in a new car. As he shopped he became disgusted with the manner of pricing which included the "optional equipment," but he made his purchase. Some time later, the salesman who sold him the car came to the farm to buy a cow. The farmer showed him several cows and helped him to decide on a particular one. Scribbling on a piece of paper, the farmer gave him an itemized bill:

Basic Cow	$200.00
Two-tone exterior	45.00
Extra stomach	75.00
Product storage compartment	60.00
Dispensing device (4 spigots @ $10 each)	40.00
Genuine cowhide upholstery	125.00
Automatic fly swatter	35.00
Dual horns	15.00
TOTAL (excluding tax & delivery)	$595.00

A lady called on a Scottish businessman to solicit money. She handed him a card that read: "Charity Fair--Give Till It Hurts." The Scotsman read it carefully and genuine tears seemed to well up in his eyes as he handed back her card: "Lady," he said, "the verra idea hurts."

In *MOTLEY'S CREW*, the pastor says, "And so on this beautiful Easter Sunday, as the collection basket is passed among you, I ask you to recall the words of the Bible, 'Render unto Caesar the things which are Caesar's and unto God the things that are God's.'"
Worshipper: "Hey, Mike, how come you smile when you render unto God but not when you render unto Caesar?"
Mike whispers: "God doesn't audit."

Pastor to delinquent member: "Don't you think you owe the Lord something?" "Yes," said the member, "But He isn't pushing me the way some of my other creditors are."

Some of us are like the big Presbyterian Church where they took up a special offering one evening for missions. They received in the offering plate $200.03. When the pastor saw those three pennies in the offering plate he chuckled and said, "We must have a Scotchman here tonight."

From the front of the balcony, a lonely voice said, "Hootman. There are three of us present."

Preparing a message on the subject 'Why We Give' made me think of a story that Dennis Hensley told on himself. Working as a chaplain's assistant at the Fort Knox Reception Station, he says that he got used to countless new recruits coming into his office with complaints on adjustments to Army life. During this initial week the recruits had to "donate" a pint of blood. One afternoon a man came storming into his office yelling, "I can't take it! They cut off all my hair, took away my civilian clothes. I mean, what do they want from a guy--blood?"

"Oh, no," Hensley assured him. "That's not until tomorrow." ∞ *The Inspirational Writer*

It happened a few days after the disastrous earthquake in Mexico City. A little boy was going door-to-door in Los Angeles selling picture postcards for twenty-five cents each. He was giving the profits for earthquake relief. One man bought some post cards from the little boy, and then he asked the boy how much he hoped to raise. The little boy answered quickly, "One million dollars!" The man smiled and said, "Do you mean to tell me that you are trying to raise a million dollars to help the earthquake victims all by yourself?" "Oh no, sir," replied the boy, "my little brother is helping me!"

A man made a financial appeal to W.C. Fields. Fields responded that he would have to confer with his lawyer. If his lawyer said yes, Fields said he would get another lawyer.

GOD

There is a story about a little fellow named Johnny who was having a dispute with his mother about green beans. Johnny's mother was trying her best to persuade the boy to eat his green beans, but he wouldn't budge. Finally, in desperation, she said, "Johnny, if you don't eat your green beans, God will punish you."

Still Johnny refused, and his mother sent him to bed. Soon, a great storm arose. Lightning flashed, great claps of thunder shook the house, and torrents of rain fell. Johnny's mother rushed upstairs to comfort her son. "Johnny, are you okay?" she asked. "I guess so," he replied, "but this sure is an awful fuss to make about a few green beans."

A church choir was raising money to attend a music competition and decided to have a car wash. To their dismay, after a busy morning, the rain began pouring down in mid-afternoon, and the customers stopped coming. Finally one of the women printed this poster: *"WE WASH,"* (and with an arrow pointed skyward) *"HE RINSES!"* Business was soon booming once again.

Woody Allen once said that he would have no difficulty believing in God. All God would have to do would be to deposit $1,000,000 in a secret Swiss bank account in Woody's name.

Lee Trevino was involved in a humorous incident in a PGA tournament sometime back. Lightning struck a tree very near to where he was standing. Someone asked Trevino what he thought when lightning struck that tree. He replied, "I learned that when God wants to play through you had better let him."

I remember a sequence on *ALL IN THE FAMILY* several years ago in which Archie Bunker is arguing with "the Meathead"--his son-in-law, a professed agnostic. The son-in-law asks, "Archie, if there is a God, why is there so much suffering in the world?" There is a long, awkward silence. Finally Archie yells, "Edith, would you get in here and help me? I'm having to defend God all by myself."

In the cartoon *BLOOM COUNTY,* little Oliver Wendall Holmes is sitting on the edge of the fence looking at the moon and stars.

Suddenly, the stars spell out: "Repent, Oliver!"

Oliver thinks, "Bloody difficult being an agnostic these days."

It is difficult to imagine how frustrated God must often be with the sort of stewardship we practice. Mark Twain imagined that God must look upon us with a sort of righteous indignation, saying something like, "Oh, this infernal human race! I wish I had it in the ark again--with an auger!"

A little boy on the Art Linkletter show years ago answered the ancient question of which came first--the chicken or the egg. "The chicken had to come first," he said, "because God can't lay eggs." His answer is probably as good as any other.

We are like the little girl who was afraid to go to bed in the dark by herself. After three or four trips to her parents' bedroom, her father sought to reassure her. "Look, honey," he said. "You are not really alone in your bedroom. God is watching over you. God is everywhere and He is in your bedroom, too." The little girl was not very reassured by this. She started back to her room but stopped at the door and said in a loud whisper, "God, if you are in there, please don't say anything. It would scare me to death."

GRATITUDE

In *BEETLE BAILEY*, the General has just set his "mess" tray down on the table, looks at it, and says grace: "Oh, Lord, for what we are about to receive, make us truly thankful." He looks at the tray again and then looks up and says, "I guess I'm not getting through, am I?"

It was Thanksgiving Day and the town grouch was grumbling as usual. "Don't you have anything to be thankful for?" a neighbor asked. "Nope," he said. "Have you considered thanking God for turning your nose right side up? He could have put it upside down. Then when it rained you would have drowned and when you sneezed, you would have blown your thankless head off."

Each of us has a different list of things for which we are thankful. A Sunday School teacher asked her class to make such a list, and a little boy wrote down that he was thankful for his glasses. The teacher was impressed by that. Some young people resent wearing glasses. Here, obviously, was a young man mature enough to appreciate what wearing glasses did for him. "Johnny," she said, "I see that you put your glasses down at the head of the list of things for which you are thankful. Is there any special reason?" Johnny answered, "Yes, ma'am. My glasses keep the boys from hitting me and the girls from kissing me."

I like the story of a brother and sister who were playing in the cow pasture when suddenly the old milk cow lost her temper and dashed for the two children. Because she was older and bigger, the sister was able to climb the nearest tree, but Johnny ran for the fence. Perched on a limb, the sister screamed out her advice, "Run, Johnny! Run!" As he neared the fence, she yelled, "Slide, Johnny! Slide!" He did, but his pants became caught in the barbed wire. Her last bit of advice was, "Pray, Johnny! Pray!" The only prayer Johnny had ever heard was his father repeating grace at mealtime, but the old cow was closing in fast and he needed to do something, so he used daddy's prayer: "Lord, we thank thee for that which we are about to receive."

Finley Peter Dunne (1867-1936), the American humorist who wrote thick dialect humor under the pseudonym of "Mr. Dooley," once said of Thanksgiving: " 'Twas founded by th' Puritans to give thanks f'r being presarved from th' Indyans, an'...we keep it to give thanks we are presarved fr'm th' Puritans."

GREATNESS

There's a little-known story about Joe Louis that I tell occasionally to show what self-control he had. He and the late G.I. comedian, Harvey Stone, were on tour entertaining the troops during the Second World War, and in their uniforms they often went unnoticed by civilians. In New York City one day they were rushing to a performance when the Brown Bomber accidentally side-swiped a cab. The irate taxi driver made tracks to Joe's open window and began hurling abuse on him that covered every racial slur in the book. As the heavy-weight champ of the world took it all in, the driver challenged him to a fight, uniform or no uniform. But Joe kept his cool and soon the frustrated cabbie drove off. Stone was flabbergasted. "Joe, why didn't you take at least one tiny swing at him for all that maligning?" Joe replied, "If someone insulted Enrico Caruso, would he have sung him an aria?" ∞Joe Franklin, *A Gift for People* (New York: M. Evans and Company, Inc., 1971).

Sugar Ray Leonard, the prize fighter, told a group of students at Harvard, "I consider myself blessed. I consider you blessed. We've all been blessed with God-given talents. Mine just happens to be beatin' people up."

Edward Streichen once said of the poet Carl Sandburg, "When God made Carl, he didn't do anything else that day."

When Bobby Ross, head football coach at Georgia Tech, was the special teams coach of the Kansas City Chiefs in the late 1970s, his field goal kicker was Jan Stenerud. At almost every practice session, Ross would work with his kicking as the future Chief's star booted ball after ball.

One afternoon, they had a difficult time finding someone to shag Stenerud's many kicks and return them to Ross.

Even today, Ross laughs when he tells this story: "I had noticed that every day these two guys--they were kind of grubby looking--would come and watch Jan practice kicking. So I asked them if they would mind getting on the other side of the fence to shag some balls, and they said. 'Sure.'

"After a few kicks, Stenerud turned to me and in his Swedish accent said, 'Coach, do you know who that one guy is shagging balls for me?'"

"I said I didn't know.

"Stenerud: 'That's George Brett of the Kansas City Royals.'

"That probably was the most expensive ball boy in history," Ross says. ☞ *Grit*, Jan. 31 - Feb. 6, 1988, p. 7.

GUILT

Noel Coward once sent identical notes to twenty of the most prominent men in London. The note said, "All is discovered. Escape while you can." All twenty abruptly left town.

There is a story of a minister in a small town who was having trouble with his collections. So one Sunday he announced from the pulpit: "Before we pass the collection plate, I would like to request that the person who stole the chickens from Brother Smith's henhouse please refrain from giving any money to the Lord. The Lord doesn't want money from a thief." The collection plate was passed around, and for the first time in many months, everybody put something in.

There is a terrible joke about a man who won a contract to paint a small country church. The man showed up on Monday with his paint but nobody was there to supervise him. The painter was more interested in making a buck than doing a good job. So he took the paint and thinned it with two quarts of water so he wouldn't have to use so much paint. He painted like this on the first side of the church then began the second. Still nobody had shown up to supervise him so he took the paint and thinned it even more. This was going to be a lucrative job. He had hardly used any paint.

Late in the day he began the third side of the church. He looked around and saw that nobody was watching him so he got ready to thin the paint out even more. Suddenly, without any warning, a booming voice split the heavens, knocking the crooked painter off the ladder. And the painter heard from the sky, "*REPAINT AND THIN NO MORE.*"

A man went to a doctor. He had been misbehaving and his conscience was bothering him. So he said to the doctor, "Will you prescribe something that will help?"

The doctor said, "Well, I don't know what I can give you to stop you from misbehaving."

The man said, "I don't want anything to stop me from misbehaving, I want something to weaken my conscience."

A fellow was telling a friend of an experience when he nearly drowned in a lake. "As I was going down for the third time," he said, "all the sins of my past life flashed before my mind."

"What did you do?" asked the friend.

"Well, after they rescued me, I jumped in again to see the show for a second time!"

There is always some risk in attempting humor--sometimes it backfires. For example, a radio disc jockey reported that at work one night he accidentally bumped the record player, sending the needle screeching across the record. To ease his error, he immediately grabbed the microphone and shouted, "Okay--which one of you listeners out there bumped into your radio and made my record skip?" To his embarrassment, several people actually phoned the radio station to apologize.

Richard Nixon was asked the greatest lesson he learned from Watergate. His response: "Just destroy all the tapes."

A policeman watched as a young man backed his car around the block. Then he did it again, and again. Finally the policeman stopped him and asked him why he was driving backward. At first the youth didn't want to explain the reasons for his strange behavior, but eventually he admitted that he had borrowed his father's car for the evening and because he had driven farther than he had promised his father that he would drive, he was backing up to try to take some of the miles off the odometer.

In *HOW TO BE A JEWISH MOTHER* by Dan Greenberg (Random House, 1964), mothers are advised to make their sons feel guilty: "If you don't know what he's done to make you suffer, he will."

HAPPINESS

There was a *PEANUTS* cartoon years ago in which Lucy asks Charlie Brown if he has ever known anybody who was really happy. Before she can finish her sentence, however, Snoopy comes dancing on tip-toe into the frame, his nose high in the air. He dances and bounces his way across two frames of the cartoon strip. Finally, in the last frame, Lucy finishs her sentence: "Have you ever known anybody who was really happy and was still in their right mind?"

There's a delightful cartoon about a father and son walking along the street. On the side of the street next to a gutter is a mud puddle. In the cartoon the father is wading in the mud puddle and jumping up and down and shouting, "Hey, you know, this really is fun."

A pilot always looked down intently on a certain valley. "What's so interesting about that spot?" asked a fellow pilot. "See that stream? Well, when I was a kid, I used to sit down there on a log fishing. Every time an airplane flew over, I would look up and wish I were flying. Now I look down and wish I were fishing."

Some years back the editors of *PSYCHOLOGY TODAY* sent questionnaires to fifty-two thousand subscribers in an effort to determine what makes people happy. The response was somewhat confusing. One subscriber wrote back and asked to see the results of the survey. "I think I am happy," he wrote. "Would you please verify?"

Laugh and the world laughs with you; cry and it's not going to change anything but your mascara. ∞ Pamela I. Young

It was time for some Friday night fun and fellowship. The three couples decided to treat themselves to a steak dinner.

When they arrived at the steak house, they were assigned a number, sent to a crowded, noisy room and told to wait there until their number was called. As they waited, a cocktail waitress came by and said, "Welcome to happy hour, what would you like to drink?"

The three couples graciously declined anything from the bar. "Just waiting for a table," they said. Fifteen minutes later, the waitress came by again with the same invitation. Again, the couples informed her they were waiting for a table. Five minutes later she returned. One of the men had mentioned to the kindergarten teacher that their table was probably being delayed in hopes that they would order something from the bar first. So when the girl came by with her, "Welcome to happy hour" speech again, the kindergarten teacher informed her: "Girl, we are all Baptists and this is as happy as we're going to get, so tell them to get us a table!" ✑ Al Fasol, *Humor With a Halo*, Lima, Ohio: C.S.S. Publishing Co., 1989).

*H*EAVEN

Billy Graham once told about something that happened a long time ago when teachers could talk about religion in the classroom. A teacher was talking to her class of young boys, and she asked, "How many of you would like to go to heaven?" And all the hands instantly shot into the air at once, except one. She was astounded. She asked, "Charlie, you mean you don't want to go to heaven?" He said, "Sure, I want to go to heaven, but not with that bunch."

In the cartoon, *BORN LOSER* is reminiscing about his younger days in the military. He says to the two little girls hanging on to his every word:

"Yes! I survived World War II from the beachheads of Normandy to Berlin! Somebody up there must really like me."

To which one of his young listeners says, "Maybe, somebody up there doesn't want you."

I am indebted to United States District Judge Richard C. Erwin for this story. George, who had lived a riotous life on earth, made a deathbed repentance and got through the pearly gates by the skin of his teeth. After some time in heaven, George went to Saint Peter and said, "I'm not happy in heaven. The golden streets are hard on my feet. I'm tired of hearing the angels twanging on their harps. Won't you let me go to hell a little while and visit my old friends?"

Saint Peter replied, "Your request is highly irregular. But I don't want anybody in heaven to be unhappy. I'll let you visit your friends in hell, provided you return by six o'clock sharp." By Saint Peter's grace, George visited his old friends in hell and had such a joyous time with them he forgot the deadline. He didn't return to heaven until nine o'clock--three hours late. Saint Peter chastised him verbally and declared that he would be compelled to discipline George severely for ignoring the deadline.

George said, "Saint Peter, you won't have to do that. I didn't come to stay. I just came to get my clothes." ∞ Sam J. Ervin, Jr., *Humor of a Country Lawyer*, (Chapel Hill: University of North Carolina Press, 1983).

There is a delightful old French story about Acousin and Nicolette who were very much in love. When the hero was chided by a priest about his affection for Nicolette and told that he might go to hell unless he took care, Acousin replied, "OH! I don't want to go to heaven and be stuck with the old men and beggars and cripples, the pious old maids. Let me go to hell where I'll find knights and warriors and people who are bold and adventurous.

"I want to go to the place where the ladies are beautiful and gay, and where I won't be bored!" ∞ *Afterlife: The Other Side of Dying,* Morton Kelsey, Chapter IX, "What Is Heaven Like?," pp. 165-166.

A person in heaven was asked what it was like. "We get up at 4 in the morning, gather in the stars, hang out the sun, and roll the clouds around all day." "How come you have to work so hard?" "To tell the truth," said the saint, "we're a little short of help up here."

I cannot think about Heaven without thinking of Mark Twain's classic remark. Twain said that the only reason he wanted to go to Heaven was because of the climate. He would prefer Hell for the company.

William Kelly was an outstanding scholar, student of the Bible, and devoted follower of the Lord. He was once offered a position at Trinity College in Dublin--a position that would have brought him prestige and privilege. But he was not interested. Those who tendered the offer asked him, "Mr. Kelly, aren't you interested in making a name for yourself in the world?" William Kelly answered, "Yes, gentlemen, but which world?"

Dwight L. Moody used to tell a story about an optimistic and cheerful lady who was, nonetheless, a shut in, bedridden in an attic apartment on the fifth floor of a run-down building. There was no elevator in the building and here she was, lying alone in a shabby room of this run-down apartment building. One of her friends came to see her one day and brought with her another friend. The second friend was of a wealthy family. They wanted to cheer up this bedridden lady, but as you are aware, sometimes these things work in reverse.

As they entered the building, the wealthy lady was struck by the austere and depressing surroundings. As they mounted the stairs to the second floor, it was almost more than she could handle. "Such a dark and filthy place," she said to her friend.

Her friend responded, "It's better higher up!"

They climbed the stairs to the third landing. "It's even worse here," she said.

Her friend responded, "It's better higher up."

Finally they got to the fifth floor and entered the apartment, tiny and run-down, of this dear lady. But the lady's face was glowing to see her friend and she was radiating with the love of Christ in her heart. The wealthier woman could not ignore the awful surroundings and she said in a sympathetic way, not wanting to be mean, but kindly, "It must be difficult for you living here like this."

The lady smiled knowingly and said, "Yes, but it's better higher up."

HUMAN NATURE

A cartoon shows two guys sitting in prison with hash marks on the wall showing their long time there. One guy looks at the other and says, "You know, it's nice to know the world's a better place because we're here."

In *CALVIN AND HOBBES,* Hobbes is the foil for the philosophies the writer shares.

Hobbes: "You look down in the dumps."

Calvin: "I am. Moe keeps knocking me down at school for no reason. He's mean just for kicks. I sure am glad you're an animal. Animals sometimes make a lot more sense than people do."

Hobbes: "...and we're cuter, too."

Calvin: "Right, Hobbes. Good point." ∽ Bill Watterson, *Something Under The Bed is Drooling*, 1988, Universal Press Syndicate.

In another *CALVIN AND HOBBES,* Calvin and his stuffed tiger (which takes on 'life' to converse with Calvin when it is convenient) have gone to Mars because Earth is no longer suitable as a place to live.

They come upon and are frightened by a "Martian" who comes out from under a rock--and who is equally frightened of them.

Calvin: "Why do you think the Martian hid from us?"

Hobbes: "Maybe Martians don't like earthlings."

Calvin: "Don't like us?! What's not to like? There's nothing wrong with humans! Hey, you Martian! Come on out! We're not bad! We just came here because people polluted our own planet so much that...uh...what I mean, is....Um...." Calvin turns to Hobbes: "So what are you saying? That our reputation preceeded us?"

Hobbes: "Would you welcome a dog that wasn't house trained?"

With so much concern about the earth and its environment, the *MIAMI HERALD* had a cartoon by Morin, which went this way:

Picture 1--a blinding flash--"In the beginning, God created Heaven and earth..."

Picture 2--the earth--"...and He created the seas..."

Picture 3--the earth--"...and then, God made man..."

Picture 4--a garbage can--"There goes the neighborhood."

As Bill Copeland said recently in the Sarasota, Florida, *JOURNAL,* "We used to hiss at the villian; now we go out and buy his book."

Will Rogers was once asked, "What is wrong with the world?" "I don't know," he drawled. "I guess it's people." On another occasion he said "God made man a little lower than the angels. Man has been getting lower ever since."

Mark Twain once said, "Man is the creature made at the end of the week's work when God was tired."

A little boy was asked what we learn from the story of Jonah and the whale. His answer was, "People make whales sick."

HUMAN RELATIONS

Prejudice is a learned response. Leo Buscaglia tells about a friend of his whose daughter is presently attending a first grade class which is predominantly black. She loves her school and her friends. Recently she was sitting at the dinner table with her parents. Out of the blue she said, "Can I have a baby sister? And please, can she be black?"

We are told that at one time it was standard practice for some West Indies nationals to conspicuously hold their noses whenever they passed an American. Their attitude is no different than that of the man from the Midwest who was visiting New York City for the first time. Someone asked him if he would be visiting the United Nations building. He answered, "Heavens, no. Confidentially, I understand that the place is just crawling with foreigners."

Lowell Lundstrom tells a story about a devout man who invited a hobo into his home and prepared a meal for him. The wanderer watched as his host sliced the bread ever so thinly. Before they ate their meal, the Christian bowed his head and began to pray the Lord's Prayer. Before he could say more than two words, his guest interrupted him.
"Wait, mister. If God is our Father, we are brothers. Right?"
"Why, yes," said the Christian.
"All right then, brother. If we are really brothers, how about slicing the bread a little thicker?"

HUMILITY

A pastor was asked to speak for a certain charitable organization. After the meeting the program chairman handed the pastor a check. "Oh, I couldn't take this," the pastor said with some embarrassment. "I appreciate the honor of being asked to speak. You have better uses for this money. You apply it to one of those uses." The program chairman asked, "Well, do you mind if we put it into our special fund?" The pastor replied, "Of course not. What is the special fund for?" The chairman answered, "It's so we can get a better speaker next year." Life is full of humbling experiences.

There is a wonderful story about actress Joan Fontaine. Shortly after her triumph in the motion picture, *REBECCA,* she was invited to dinner at the Sam Goldwyn's home. Goldwyn's hilltop residence was the symbol of success to the Hollywood stars of that day. You had really made it when you got that invitation to "come up." Fontaine and her husband, Brian Aherne, were prepared for this summit meeting par excellence. They arrived in their finest clothes, fashionably late, only to discover that no other cars had parked in the driveway. To avoid seeming eager, they decided to drive around awhile--but still no one showed up. "Let's go home and check the invitation," Brian suggested. "We must have the wrong day." So they did, but the date and time were right. Now an hour late, they courageously made their entrance, only to discover that the Goldwyns were indeed waiting for them--for a dinner alone. ∞ Joe Franklin, *A Gift for People*, (New York: M. Evans and Company, Inc., 1971).

I heard about a certain speaker who had a speech on "humility" but was waiting to give it at a convention where a large-enough crowd would be assured.

It's great to watch reporters interview the losers after any athletic contest. Some players accept reponsibility for their loss, and some will invariably find an excuse for why they were defeated in spite of their great ability.

One of the more humble--and honest--replies came from the losing quarterback after the 1940 NFL playoffs. The Chicago Bears had just humiliated the Washington Redskins 73 to 0.

Only three weeks before, the Redskins had beaten the Bears. Naturally, reporters talked about the importance that momentum makes, and one of them asked the Redskin's quarterback how the game might have been different if his team had scored first. The quarterback replied that the score would then have been 73 to 7.

He was admitting that his team was simply outplayed that day! ∞ Jack Newcombe, editor, *The Fireside Book of Football* (New York, New York: Simon and Schuster, 1964), p. 86.

Notre Dame football coach Lou Holtz said, "I've been on the top and I've been on the bottom. At Arkansas my first year, we won the Orange Bowl. Then everybody loved me.

"They put me into the Arkansas Hall of Fame and issued a commemorative stamp in my honor. The next year we lost to Texas, and they had to take away the stamp. People kept spitting on the wrong side.

"One year I tried to sell cemetery plots for a living. My wife told me I couldn't sell anything. She was wrong. That summer, I sold our car, our television, our stereo..."

Actress Jane Wyman tells about an evening when she was entertaining very special guests. Among her detailed preparations, she put a note on the guest towels, "If you use these I will murder you." It was meant for her husband. In the excitement she forgot to remove the note. After the guests departed, the towels were discovered still in perfect order, as well as the note itself. Life would be dull without such miscues.

I recall the story of the Dominican monk who said that "The Jesuits are known for their learning, and the Francis cans for their piety and good works, but when it comes t humility, we're tops!"

One author tells us that in Los Angeles the police ar famous for their courtesy. When they stop a traffic offende they go out of their way to avoid creating more anxiety that already exists in such a situation. They don't swagger aroun with an exaggerated sense of their own importance. One res dent of that city was quite proud of never having received single traffic citation in twenty years even though he had bee stopped many times. He credited this to his practice of alway getting out of his car and meeting the officer halfway. On day, however, he was signaled to pull over on a busy L freeway. He stopped his car, started to get out, and wa stopped by a bellow from the officer: "Get back in that ca you fool!" The driver obeyed. "Sorry for yelling at you," th officer said. "Freeways are not designed for pedestrians. It' very dangerous to walk even for a short distance." Our frien commented, "How could I not cooperate with someone wh was really interested in saving my life? Why, I couldn't eve bring myself to talk my way out of a ticket!" ☞ Gerald I Nieren berg and Henry Caier, *Meta-Talk*, (New York: Cornerston Library, 1973).

Chertkov, a disciple of Tolstoy, was a wealthy aristocra Tolstoy once reprimanded him for traveling first class, sug gesting that, to demonstrate his humility, he should g second. On his next journey the obedient Chertkov hired a entire second-class coach for himself.

"If at first you don't succeed--try to hide you astonishment."

A lady was boring everyone at the table with nonstop recital of personal superiority. Hers was the towns most expensive house, most luxurious car, most successful business--ad nauseam. "And, of course," she droned on, "my ancestors came over on the Mayflower."

"How fortunate for you," smiled one member of her captive audience. "The immigration laws have been tightened considerably since then."

Senator Henry S. Foote of Mississippi was never on good terms with Senator Thomas Hart Benton. Foote once threatened to write "a little book in which Mr. Benton would figure very largely."Benton was unabashed. "Tell Foote," he said,"that I'll write a very large book in which he will not figure at all."

Woman to friend: "I've started a new diet. No more eating my own words, swallowing my pride or putting my foot in my mouth."

During the presidency of Lyndon Johnson, Bill Moyers, the President's press secretary (and a Baptist minister), was asked to offer the mealtime prayer. He began by praying quietly. President Johnson became somewhat irritated and interrupted him."Pray louder!" he said. The press secretary looked up and replied, "I'm sorry, sir, but I wasn't addressing you."

"Roy, I need some good advice," says Peppermint Patty. "What do you do when something you've counted on doesn't happen? This thing I really believed was going to happen, didn't happen. What do I do?" Says Roy, "Well, you could admit you were wrong." Replies Peppermint Patty, "Besides that, I mean."

A Texas man was bragging on the "bigness" of everything in Texas. He was surprised when an "Okie" stepped up and agreed with him. "Yes", said the Okie, "that's right, everything's big in Texas! Why, I once knew a Texan who was so big they couldn't find a coffin big enough to bury him in when he died." "And what did they do?" asked the surprised Texan. "Well," came the answer, "they just let the air out of him, and buried him in a shoebox!"

Someone wrote: "Most of us camouflage our stumbling block with a hat!"

A famous naturalist once visited fellow nature-lover Theodore Roosevelt at Sagamore Hill, Roosevelt's home. One evening the two of them walked on the lawn looking up at the stars. They talked of the galaxies and the great expanses of the universe. They identified the various constellations. Then followed silence.

Finally Teddy Roosevelt summed it all up: "Now I think we are small enough. Let's go to bed."

A million years from now the earth will probably be peopled by creatures who will stoutly deny that they ever descended from man.

"Archeologists unearthed 2 human skulls 7,000 years old with the brains largely intact and tissue containing much DNA. Perhaps in 5000 BC folks had brains very like we have in 1984, but it would be mean to say that about the folks of 5000 BC." ∽ George Will

In a *PEANUTS* comic strip, Lucy is walking along the road with Charlie Brown. Charlie Brown asks her: "Lucy, are you going to make any New Year's resolution?" Lucy hollers back at him, knocking him off his feet: "What? What for? What's wrong with me now? I like myself the way I am! Why should I change? What in the world is the matter with you, should I change? What in the world is the matter with you, Charlie Brown? I'm all right the way I am! I don't have to improve. How could I improve? How, I ask you? How?"

Howard Baker, Jr., the former senator from Tennessee and White House chief of staff, said he still remembers the advice his dad gave him after Baker argued his first case as a fledgling attorney. His dad told him, "In the future, son, I would guard against speaking more clearly than you think."

A boy got a job in the city and left the family farm. He wrote home to his older brother, trying to impress him with his new life: "Thursday we motored out to the club, where we golfed until dark. Then we motored out to the beach and weekended."

The brother, thoroughly unimpressed, wrote back: "Sunday we motored to town and baseballed all afternoon. Yesterday we muled out to the cornfield till sundown. Then we suppered. After that we staircased to our rooms and bedsteaded till the clock fived."

There is a story told of a woman who, while on a trip to China, bought an old medallion which she liked so well she began to wear it almost constantly about her neck. Its bizarre and striking design always gave rise to interested conversation; and the woman became so fond of it she adopted it as her good-luck charm.

At a diplomatic dinner in Washington she met the Chinese ambassador who, she noticed, was observing the medallion with a faint smile upon his lips. "Have you seen one of these before, Ambassador?" the lady inquired. He admitted that he had and promptly changed the subject. "Would you be so kind as to translate the inscription on it?" the lady asked. The ambassador said that he would rather not. The lady insisted. "Very well, madam," he said at last with great reluctance. "It says 'Licensed Prostitute, City of Shanghai'."
∞ Gina Cerminara, *The World Within*, p. 45.

And this is good old Boston,
The home of the bean and the cod;
Where the Lowells talk only to Cabots
And the Cabots talk only to God.
℃ John Collins Bossidy

An out-of-state visitor was being shown the ranch of a Texas friend. As they looked across the barren dusty land, a bird dashed across the yard. "That's a bird of paradise," said the Texan.

Looking around tentatively, the visitor replied, "He's a long way from home, isn't he?"

The hostess at a very elaborate dinner party was seated quite a distance from one of her guests--an actress of some fame. Seeking to help all of her guests have a more pleasant evening, she wrote a note to the actress and had the maid deliver it.

The actress couldn't read without her glasses, so she asked the man on her right to read it to her. "It says," he read, 'Darling, do me a favor and don't ignore the man on your right. I know he is a bore, but talk to him anyway.'"

There is a story about Sir David Edgeworth, the Australian geologist and explorer, who accompanied Ernest Shackleton on his expedition to the South Pole at the turn of the century. During the South Pole expedition, Sir Edgeworth's assistant, Douglas Mawson, was working in his tent one day when he heard a muffled cry from outside. "Are you very busy?" called the voice, which Mawson recognized as that of Sir Edgeworth. "Yes I am," he replied. "What's the matter?" "Are you really very busy?" "Yes," snapped Mawson, losing his patience. "What is it you want?"

After a moment's silence, Sir David replied apologetically, "Well, I'm down a crevasse, and I don't think I can hang on much longer."

I remember a story told about Albert Schweitzer who was visiting a certain city, and dignitaries were awaiting him at the train station. But he was not to be found among the first-class passengers. So they waited while the second-class passengers disembarked. Still no Schweitzer. Finally, they saw him coming out of the third-class compartment, carrying his own suitcase. "Why on earth do you travel third-class?" they asked him. "Because there is no fourth-class!" he replied.

A senator once took Will Rogers to the White House to meet President Coolidge. He warned Will that Coolidge never smiled. Will said, "I'll make him smile."

Inside the Oval Office, the senator said, "Will, I'd like you to meet President Coolidge."

Rogers said with a deadpan expression, "I'm sorry, but I didn't catch the name." Coolidge smiled. ☜ *GRIT*

John Brodie, former quarterback for the San Francisco 49ers, was once asked why a superstar like himself should have to hold the ball for field goals and points after touchdown. "Well," said Brodie, "if I didn't, the ball would fall over."

Yogi Berra read only the sports pages, so he was clearly at a loss when introduced to novelist Ernest Hemingway in a restaurant. Someone asked Berra if he had ever heard of the famous author. "I don't think so," Berra admitted. "What paper does he write for?"

IDENTITY

A cartoon pictured a man whose physician examined him and said, "You have a very serious problem. You are allergic to yourself."

After many years in an institution, a mental patient was discharged. But he was very unhappy. "You're cured," said his doctor. "Some cure," the healed man pouted. "When I first came here, I was Abraham Lincoln. Now I'm nobody!"

A man was arrested as a horse thief. "Do you plead innocent or guilty?" he was asked.
"Innocent, of course."
"Do you want to be tried by a judge or a jury of your peers?"
"What are peers?" he asked.
"People just like you," said the judge.
His retort: "What, me be tried by a bunch or horse thieves? Never."

I like what Sam Levenson once said: "I pay my psychiatrist sixty dollars an hour and all he does is ask me the same question my father used to ask me all the time-- 'Who do you think you are anyway?'"

I am reminded of a soldier who was trying to get a check cashed in the small town near the base to which he had been assigned.
"I'm sorry," said the merchant who was waiting on him, "but I can't cash your check without some kind of identification. Haven't you got any friends at the base who could vouch for you?"
"Not me," the soldier answered. "I'm the camp's bugler."

Psychological therapist Richard Bandler tells about visiting a mental institution and dealing with a man who insisted he was Jesus Christ. One day Bandler walked in to meet with this man. "Are you Jesus?" Bandler asked. "Yes, my son," the man replied. Bandler said, "I'll be back in a minute." This left the man a little bit confused. Within three or four minutes, Bandler came back, holding a measuring tape. Asking the man to hold out his arms, Bandler measured the length of his arms and his height from head to toe. After that, Bandler left. The man claiming to be Christ became a little concerned. A little while later, Bandler came back with a hammer, some large spiked nails, and a set of long boards. He began to pound them into the form of a cross. The man asked, "What are you doing?" As Bandler put the last nails in the cross, he asked, "Are you Jesus?" Again the man answered, "Yes, my son." Bandler said, "Then you know why I am here." Suddenly the man had a remarkable recovery.

"I'm not Jesus. I'm not Jesus!" the man started yelling.
☞ Brennan Manning, *Lion and Lamb*, (Old Tappan, N.J.: Fleming H. Revell, 1986).

A woman got on an elevator in a tall office building. There was just one other person in the elevator, a handsome man. She pushed the button for her floor and then casually looked over at the man and suddenly had one of those moments of recognition shock. Could it be? The man looked exactly like Robert Redford, the movie star. Her gaze was almost involuntarily riveted on him. Finally she blurted out, "Are you the REAL Robert Redford?" He smiled and said, "Only when I'm alone!"

At the end of Woody Allen's brilliant film on human relationships, *ANNIE HALL*, Woody tells an old story about the man who thought he was a chicken. His wife went to a psychiatrist for some help in dealing with her husband's problem. After she had explained her husband's behavior to the doctor he said, "That's ridiculous! Why don't you tell him he's not a chicken?" The woman immediately responded, "Because I need the eggs!"

One of the great press agents was the late Dexter Fellows who worked for Ringling Brothers and Barnum and Bailey. He took great pride in the "greatest show on earth." Once he entered a newspaper office in the Midwest and simply announced, "I am Dexter Fellows of the circus."

One clerk looked up and asked, "What circus?"

"Good Heavens, man," he cried out, with all the horror o
sacrilege on his face, "if you were in London and heard a man
say, 'God Save the King,' would you interrupt him and ask
what king?"

Sol M. Linowitz, a prominent lawyer, once told a story
about William Howard Taft's great-granddaughter. When she
was asked to write her autobiography in the third grade, the
young lady responded: "My great-grandfather was President
of the United States, my grandfather was a United States
senator; my father is an ambassador; and I am a brownie."

At the Goethe Festival at Aspen, Colorado, in 1949, Or
tega y Gasset is said to have crossed to the great auditorium
immediately after breakfast one morning and as he entered
a woman stepped up to him and said, "Is this Mr. Ortega?"

The Spanish existentialist philosopher gazed at her
paused for a moment, and then replied, "No, Madam. Just a
poor inadequate representation of the authentic Ortega."

JUDGMENT

Have you noticed that a lot of people seem to have
graduated from "Bumper Sticker Seminary?" They proclaim
their theological position on their cars. One bumper sticker
says: "Christ is coming again, and boy! Is He mad!" Another
says: "Jesus is coming again! Look busy!"

Years ago I heard about a Kansas preacher who
returned home after visiting New England.

One of his parishioners met him at the train.

"Well," asked the preacher, "how are things at home?"

"Sad, real sad, pastor. A cyclone came and wiped out my house."

"Well, I'm not surprised," said the rather blunt parson with a frown. "You remember I've been warnin' you about the way you've been livin'. Punishment for sin is inevitable."

"It also destroyed your house, sir," added the layman.

"It did?" The pastor was horrified. "Ah me, the ways of the Lord are past human understanding."

A man who had been a rascal most of his life was in the hospital for surgery. Coming out from under the anesthetic, he found that the blinds to his hospital room were drawn. He complained to the nurse that he could not see out and asked why they were drawn in the first place. "Oh, calm down," said the nurse. "There's a big fire burning across the street, and we didn't want you to wake up and think that the operation was a failure!"

Aren't you glad salvation doesn't work like it is pictured in a recent magazine cartoon? In it two men dressed in business suits, one carrying a briefcase, are standing in the clouds of heaven at the desk of St. Peter, who has a pen out and the book of eternal life open. Evidently, Peter is preparing to hear their reason for entering the Kingdom.

One of the men says, "My name is Howard C. Freswell, and this is Arthur Templeton, my attorney." ☞ *Christianity Today*

In 1860 a French chemist named Marcellin Berthelot prophesied that "within a hundred years...man will know what the atom is. It is my belief that when science reaches this stage, God will come down to earth with his big ring of keys and will say to humanity, 'Gentlemen, it's closing time.'" ☞ Quoted in The New York Times, October 2, 1970

JUSTICE

Here's a story that can really work: "I was on an airplane flight home one afternoon. I sat in the non-smoking section. I was seated on the aisle of the plane. After the plane had taken off the man across from me took out one of those little short cigars that look like compressed leather. He lit up and started puffing noxious black smoke into the air. This really bugged me. I leaned across the aisle and said politely, "I'm sorry, sir, but this is the non-smoking section. You can't smoke here." The smoker just ignored me, and looked straight ahead as if no one else in the world existed. Finally I decided I had had enough and called for the stewardess. This lovely stewardess came down the aisle and asked, "Can I help you?" I said, "Yes, this man is ignoring the non-smoking section and smoking that awful thing!" The stewardess said to the smoker, "I'm sorry, sir, but this is the non-smoking section and you can't smoke here. There are some seats in the back, if you would like. But in any case you can't smoke cigars anywhere on the plane." The man ignored her and kept puffing on his cigar. The stewardess went to the back of the plane, exasperated. Later in the flight, the plane began to run into some turbulence. Just as the stewardess passed the cigar-smoker, the plane hit an air pocket and she spilled her entire tray of beverages on the man, effectively extinguishing his foul cigar. Then, reacting to her fall, she leaned back and fell right into my lap! Don't tell me there's no God!"

The tired businessman said to the attorney, "I'll hire you --if you're positive I'll win the case."

"Well," said the attorney, "Let's hear the facts."

The businessman launched into a detailed account of a scandalized partnership, ending with, "Now, can I sue and get my money back?"

"Absolutely!" said the attorney. "I've rarely heard such an open-and-shut case."

The businessman groaned. "What's the matter?" asked the attorney.

"I just told you *HIS* side of the story."

I like the story of a man who had been caught driving 40 miles per hour in a school zone. He was fined $100. The clerk offered him a receipt when he paid his fine. "Why would I want a receipt for a traffic violation?" the man growled.

"Oh," the clerk replied, "with four of these you get a bicycle to ride."

$\mathcal{K}$NOWLEDGE

Once there was a young fellow who was in a class studying the multiplication table. The teacher asked him to recite the nines. The boy stumbled along and did not do very well. Finally he said, "Teacher, I don't know the nines very well, but I'm a tiger when it comes to the sevens."

Writer Alex Haley's uncle, a rather self-satisfied person, always wore his Phi Beta Kappa key on a chain around his neck. Another of Haley's relatives, a woman of a realistic turn of mind, eyed the key, and said, "Real pretty. But what does it unlock?"

There is an old story of a boilermaker who was hired to fix a huge steamship boiler system. After listening to the engineer's description of the problems and asking a few questions, he went to the boiler room. He looked at the maze of twisting pipes, listened to the thump of the boiler and the hiss of escaping steam for a few minutes, and felt some pipes with his hands. Then he hummed softly to himself, reached into his overalls and took out a small hammer, and tapped a bright red valve, once. Immediately the entire system began working perfectly, and the boilermaker went home. When the steamship owner received a bill for $1000, he complained that the boilermaker had only been in the engine room for fifteen minutes, and requested an itemized bill: *FOR TAPPING WITH HAMMER -- .50. FOR KNOWING WHERE TO TAP -- $999.50*

There is a terrible story about a man whose wife had a cat which the man despised. The cat was always under his feet, always leaving scratch marks on the furniture, always shedding cat hairs on the man's trousers. Finally, while his wife was visiting her mother one weekend, the man took the cat out and drowned it. His wife was in hysterics when she returned to find her cat gone. To comfort her, the husband made the grand gesture of taking out an ad in the newspapers and offering $1,000 for the cat's safe return. A friend who heard about the man's offer said, "Man, you're crazy. That's a huge reward to offer for a cat." The man smiled and replied, "When you know what I know, you can afford to take the risk."

One applicant for a police force failed to get a passing grade on the written exam. However, because he was a relative of the chief, the examiner gave him an easy question to start the oral exam: "Who shot Abraham Lincoln?"

The applicant hesitated and finally asked if he could have a little time to give his answer. The examiner shrugged resignedly and instructed him to report back the next morning.

When the would-be cop arrived home, his wife anxiously inquired if he had gotten the job.

"I think so," he told her, " 'cause they got me workin' on a case already." ☜ *American Legion Magazine*

As someone has said, "Never try to teach a pig to sing. It wastes your time and it annoys the pig."

I like something I once read about Harry Truman. A friend of President Truman arrived early in the morning and the President wasn't up yet, but Mrs. Truman said, "Go right into his bedroom--he'd love to see you." So his friend, a prominent publisher, walked in, and there was the former President, sitting in a big chair with two stacks of new books on either side of him. He had obviously just gone out and bought all those books. His friend said, "Mr. President, as a publisher, I'm so pleased to see that you are buying all those books. I suppose you read yourself to sleep at night." Harry Truman answered, "No, young man, I read myself *AWAKE*." ∽ David McCullough, *The Unexpected Harry Truman*.

On his deathbed, the great philosopher Hegel complained, "Only one man ever understood me." He fell silent for a while and then added, "And he didn't understand me."

At her citizenship hearing in 1967, Immaculata Cuomo (mother of Mario Cuomo) was asked by the judge how many stars were on the U.S. flag. She said she didn't know, but could she ask the judge a question? After he agreed, she asked him how many hands of bananas were on a stalk. He admitted he didn't know, so she proudly said, "Well, I do." Her citizenship was granted. ∽ Quoted in *Atlantic Monthly*, March, 1988.

John Wesley was, perhaps, the most brilliant man of the 18th century. He read eight languages, wrote some 440 books and pamphlets, and had an intellectual curiosity far beyond any of his peers. But not everyone was impressed. One woman wrote to him: "Mr. Wesley, I have been instructed by the Lord to tell you that He has no need of your learning." To which Wesley replied, "Madame, while I have no direct word from the Lord on this matter, I feel constrained to tell you that the Lord has no need of your ignorance, either!"

A farmer was approached by a young county farm agent who tried to convince him of the value of scientific methods in the production of crops. Exasperated, the farmer said, "See here, young feller, don't you come around here telling me how to farm. I done wore out three farms already."

Never lend books, for no one ever returns them; the only books I have in my library are books that other folks have lent me. ∞ Anatole France

A farmer and a college professor were traveling together on a train. After a few days, they got tired of talking and reading, so the professor suggested they play riddles. "Every time you miss a riddle, you give me a dollar, and if I miss a riddle, I'll give you a dollar," said the professor.

"You're better educated than I am," the farmer pointed out, "so I'll give you fifty cents."

The professor agreed, and the farmer made up the first riddle.

"What has three legs walking and two legs flying?"

The professor didn't know, so he gave the farmer a dollar.

The farmer didn't know either, so he gave the professor fifty cents. ∞ *Woodmen of the World*

It has been said that Aristotle was the last Western thinker that could actually know all that there was to be known. Before his time there wasn't much to know; and after him there was far too much.

Two American ladies in Paris were chatting. One said, "I've been here more than a week now and I haven't been to the Louvre." The other replied, "Neither have I. It must be the water." ∞Jerome Beatty, *Saturday Review*

LANGUAGE

A mouse was being chased by a large cat. At the last possible moment, she dashed into her hole to find her children cowering in the corner. The cat, unsatisfied, remained growling and clawing at the hole. Suddenly, the mother mouse raised herself up on her hind legs and barked exactly like a dog. The cat turned tail and fled. The danger gone, the mouse turned to her children and said, "Now children, you have learned the value of being bilingual."

In speech, the Chinese have no sound for "r," and the Japanese have no sound for "l." You have to be careful with ethnic humor, but I don't believe anyone could be offended by this little gem making the rounds:

A factory owner decided to hire more ethnic personnel. He hired a German, an Irishman, and a Chinese. He put the German in charge of production and the Irishman in charge of personnel. Then the owner turned to the Chinese and said, "Wong, I'm putting you in charge of supplies."

Three weeks later the owner returned to the factory to see how things were going.

"Vunderful!" answered the German.

"Bless me now, things couldn't be better!" exclaimed the Irishman.

"Where is Wong?" the owner asked the two workers. They didn't know.

The owner, perplexed, began a search throughout the factory. Unsuccessful, he turned to leave, and just as he was walking out the door, the Chinese man leaped out from behind a large stack of boxes and yelled, "SUPPLIES!"

It is no "supplies" why things are going so badly right now...

LEADERSHIP

I read about a cartoon that appeared in a magazine sometime back showing a little boy attempting to lead a huge Saint Bernard dog on a leash. The dog was dragging the boy along behind and obviously in a direction different from which the boy wanted to go. The young fellow was bracing his feet and angrily shouting to the dog, "Let's get this straight! You are my dog. I am not your boy!"

Harold Geneen, the dynamic businessman, has always been something of an enigma. Long after he had been running ITT, he remained a mystery man to such an extent that the press often misprinted his name as Geheen or Green. People in his own company were not even certain how to pronounce his name. There was a joke about it inside ITT: "Is the 'G' hard as in God, or soft as in Jesus?"

During World War II industrialist Henry J. Kaiser was brought to Washington, D.C., to testify concerning his ship building activities. He had claimed to be able to build a ship a day. He was being cross-examined by a somewhat hostile young lawyer who said, "So you think you can build a ship a day. You know, Rome wasn't built in a day."

Henry J. Kaiser looked the young lawyer squarely in the eye and answered, "I wasn't there."

LIMITS

Some of our limits exist only in our own minds. A couple of years ago, during a sports clinic at Princeton High School in Cincinnati, Ohio, Dan Woodruff, the softball coach, lent his office to Dave Redding, the "strength" coach for the Cleveland

Browns. Dave wanted to shower before his scheduled appearance at the clinic.

Dan showed Dave the facilities, then left while he was in the shower. When Dave finished showering, he went to leave the office, but found he couldn't open the door! He wrote a note and slipped it under the door, then sat back and waited.

When Dan went back to his office about an hour later, he heard someone yelling, "Help, help!" Then he found the card outside his door. He opened the door and found Redding. "What's the problem?" Dan asked. Dave told him that he had been locked inside for over an hour. Dan told him the door wasn't locked, that he had only to push a button on the handle to make it open.

"We laughed about it a lot when we walked down the hall," said Dan. "The 230 pound strength coach of a professional football team being trapped behind an unlocked door."

LOSER

Charlie Brown, Linus, and Lucy are on their way to school. Lucy asks Linus if he has remembered to bring anything for show-and-tell that day.

"Yes," Linus answers, "I have a couple of things here to show the class." He then unfolds some papers. "These are copies I've been making of some of the Dead Sea scrolls," he says. Holding them up for Charlie Brown and Lucy to inspect, he continues. "This is a duplicate of the scroll of Isaiah, chapters 38-40. It was made from 17 pieces of sheep skin and was found in a cave by a Bedouin shepherd."

Pulling out another piece of paper he says, "Here I have made a copy of the earliest known fragment ever found. It's a portion of I Samuel 23: 9-16. I'll try to explain to the class how these manuscripts have influenced modern scholarship."

Lucy responds, "Very interesting, Linus," and she turns to Charlie Brown, who has a frustrated expression on his face, and asks, "Are you bringing something for show-and-tell, Charlie Brown?"

"Well," says a dejected Charlie Brown, "I had a little red fire engine here but I think I'll just forget it."

In a *PEANUTS* strip Lucy is parked in her psychiatric booth, and Charlie Brown is sharing his problems with her. "Sometimes I ask myself questions," he begins. "Sometimes I ask myself, 'Is this your real life, or is this just a pilot film? Is my life a thirty-nine-week series or is it something special?'" In no time at all Lucy analyzes his problem and gives an instant answer: "Whatever it is, you ratings are down. Five cents, please."

One comedian moaned, "I overslept this morning and in the rush to get started, I ruined my toast, spilled coffee all over my suit, and cut myself shaving. My neighbor's dog bit me while I was rushing to my car, which wouldn't start...From there, the day seemed to go downhill!"

A writer with a real sense of humor put it like this: "You know it's going to be a bad day when...
--You call your answering service and they tell you it's none of your business.
--Your horn goes off accidentally and remains stuck as you follow a group of Hell's Angels on the freeway.
--You sink your teeth into a beautiful steak and they stay there.
--The moving van starts to unload next door and the first four things down the ramp are motorcycles.
--Your 14-year-old daughter insists that Jesus never preached against pierced noses.
--Your church treasurer says, 'The IRS called me the other day about some of your donation totals!'"

One fellow was asked by an acquaintance, "What are you thinking of, my friend? You look so depressed."
"My future," came the reply.

"Well, what makes it look so hopeless and dismal?" asked his friend.

"My past," he replied glumly.

We are like three burglars I read about who reportedly tried to open a safe in a small factory in Vang, Norway. They attached an explosive device to the door and hid in the next room until it went off. Unfortunately, the explosion was so powerful it demolished the entire building and buried them under a pile of rubble. The safe contained no money—it contained explosives.

When some future generation tries to understand the spirit of our times, an unknown scholar might run across a collection of the many derivatives of Murphy's law:

"If anything can go wrong it will. If nothing can go wrong, it will anyway.

"Nothing is as easy as it looks.

"Everything takes longer than you think.

"The other line always moves faster.

"The probability of a peanut butter sandwich falling on the carpet face side up is directly proportional to the cost of the carpet.

"The light at the end of the tunnel is probably an oncoming train."

And that real clincher: "Murphy was an optimist."

Murphy's Law was amply illustrated in a joke that went around sometime back about a man who was crawling through the desert on his hands and knees, desperate for a drink of water. He encountered a man selling neckties. "Would you like to buy a nice necktie?" the salesman asked. "All I want is a drink of water," the man growled. The salesman had no water, so the poor man kept crawling across the sand. Miraculously, out in the middle of that vast desert, he came upon a beautiful restaurant. At first he thought it was a mirage, but as he moved closer he saw that it was real. With his last ounce of energy he struggled up to the entrance and said to the doorman, "Please, I must have a drink of water." To which the doorman replied, "Sorry, gentlemen are not admitted without neckties."

A young woman went away to college in the fall, leaving her plants and her goldfish in the care of her mother, who had a tendency to be forgetful. Some of us may know somebody with a "brown thumb." This mother had one. The plants that the daughter left behind in the care of her mother died at the end of the month. The mother dutifully broke the bad news to her. When the young woman called a week later, her mother confessed that the goldfish had died too. There was a long pause, then in a fearful voice the girl asked, "How's Dad?"

A young man went ice fishing for the first time in his life. He arrived with all his equipment and began to cut a circle in the ice. Suddenly he heard a deep voice say somberly, "Don't cut that ice." The young man stopped, looked around, didn't see anyone, so he moved to a different part of the ice and started to drill another circle. Again the deep voice from nowhere announced, "Don't cut that ice." Finally the young man yelled, "All right, what's going on here? What are you bothering me for? Just who the heck do you think you are anyway?" To which the mystery voice replied, "I'm manager of this skating rink!"

You may have heard the story about a man whose farm was failing, whose wife needed surgery, and whose bills were past due. The banks wouldn't lend him a cent. He decided to take a short-cut. He decided to rob a bank. He knew it was wrong but he was desperate. He tried to gain enough courage. He paced back and forth in front of the bank. He had a bag for the teller to put the money in and a pistol with which to frighten her. Finally he decided to do it. Shakily, he walked into the bank, rushed right up to a teller, handed the gun to her, pointed the bag at her and stammered, "Don't stick with me--this is a mess up!"

Notre Dame football coach, Lou Holtz, is noted for his sense of humor as well as for winning football teams.

This one he told the annual sales meeting of the Western Insurance Companies:

One night a guy is driving home from a party and he's pulled over by a cop. The cop said, "Sir, you were driving 77."

The guy said, "No, I wasn't. I had it on Cruis-a-matic. I was driving 55."

Cop: "Sorry, sir. My radar said '77'."

The guy said, "Officer, I'm going to have your job, your badge, and then, I'm going to punch you in the nose."

The cop turned to the man's wife and said, "Is he always like this?"

The wife replied, "Only when he's drunk."

Poor Charlie Brown can't do anything right. Lucy doesn't help. On one occasion she puts her hands on her hips and says, "You, Charlie Brown, are a foul ball in the line drive of life! You're the shadow of your own goal posts! You are a miscue! You are three putts on the eighteenth green! You are a seven-ten split in the tenth frame; a love set! You have dropped a rod and a reel in the lake of life! You are a missed free throw, a shanked nine iron and a called third strike! Do you understand? Have I made myself clear?"

There is a ridiculous story that they are telling in the oil fields in Texas. It is about a man named Johnson who was a powerful and successful business executive. One day he invested in a tax shelter that promised a five-to-one write-off. It turned out to be a fraud, and Johnson lost $200,000. To make things worse, his business associates lost their respect for him, and the IRS decided to audit his finances. Depressed, he threw himself on the couch in his office and cried out, "Lord, I make million-dollar decisions every day and almost never make a mistake. Why did you make me look like such an idiot this time?"

Suddenly there was a clap of thunder and a brilliant light appeared in the center of the room. A loud, powerful voice said, "Don't cry about your problems. I had half a million invested in that deal, too."

Canines and cars don't mix! Dateline, Norwalk, Connecticut. Police are accustomed to hearing outlandish excuses for accidents, but the one they heard from Joseph Vellone was a new wrinkle.

Vellone told police the reason his car ran into a building was because his dog took over the vehicle. Vellone said he was driving along a Norwalk street with the dog, an 8-month-old, mixed-breed shepherd named Ebony, riding in the front seat beside him.

When Vellone had to stop for a red light, he opened his door to spit. The dog bumped into Vellone and knocked him into the street, and the car rolled through the intersection toward a utility pole and a building with Vellone in frantic pursuit.

But the car struck the building before Vellone could catch it. Fortunately, the building was undamaged, and the car sustained only minor damage, police said. The dog also came through the incident unscathed, but Vellone received a minor abrasion on his left leg. The damage to his dignity was a good bit more severe.

A fellow was driving home in a very dense fog. The only objects he could see clearly were the taillights of the car ahead, so he decided for the sake of safety to just follow those lights to be certain that he stayed on the road. Suddenly, without warning, the taillights ahead came to a complete stop and he ran into the driver he had been following. "Why didn't you give some kind of signal that you were going to stop?" he shouted angrily at the other driver. "Why should I?" came the reply, "I was in my own garage!"

There is a ridiculous story about a wealthy Texan who died, and his attorney gathered the entire family for the reading of the will. Relatives came from near and far to see if they were included in the bequests. The lawyer somberly opened the will and began to read:

"To my cousin Ed, I leave my ranch.

"To my brother Jim, I leave my money market accounts.

"To my neighbor and good friend, Fred, I leave my stocks.

"And finally, to my cousin George, who always sat around and never did anything, but wanted to be remembered in my will, I want to say, 'Hi, George.'"

Dr. John Ziegler of Cincinnati, Ohio, sent for a government publication called Handbook for Emergencies. He enclosed the number of the government publication, #15,700. Two weeks later Dr. John Ziegler received 15,700 copies of the booklet that he had ordered.

A football coach was quizzing his players. With fire in his eyes he marched up to a seldom used third-string offensive tackle and posed this possibility. "Suppose," said the coach, "We were involved in a tie game. One minute remained. We were three yards from the goal line and a play was called to the left side of the line. What would you do?" The lineman thought for a moment and answered, "Gee, Coach, I don't know. I reckon I would slide down the bench to get a better view."

A hill-billy cafe was caught putting horse meat in their rabbit stew.

State food inspector: "How much horse meat did you put in the rabbit stew?"

Cook: "Oh, we made it 50/50."

Inspector: "How's that?"

Cook: "We put one horse to one rabbit." ☜Wade Burton

Sometime back in Sydney, Australia, a prisoner succeeded in escaping jail. He hid in the underpinnings of a delivery truck that had stopped briefly in the prison warehouse. He held on desperately as the truck drove out of the prison. A few moments later, when the truck stopped, the prisoner dropped down to the ground and rolled outward to freedom. Unfortunately he discovered that he was now in the courtyard of another prison five miles from the first.

"Life," E.M. Forster wrote, "is a public performance on the violin, in which you must learn the instrument as you go along."

Life is like an airliner I heard about recently that was making its way from New York to San Francisco. One of the engines caught fire. The captain came on the speaker system, calmly reassuring the people that the fire would soon be out. Besides, the plane could fly just as well with three engines as with four.

Unfortunately, a second engine burst into flames. Once again the captain spoke to the passengers, saying that two engines were sufficient. But then, a third engine was suddenly ablaze. The captain said no more. There was only silence from the front of the plane. Soon the captain appeared in the cabin with a parachute on his back. Just before he opened the exit door, he said calmly to the passengers, "Don't anyone panic, I'm going for help." And out he jumped.

Mother Nature couldn't make us perfect, so she did the next best thing--she made us blind to our faults.

Samuel Chadwick said, "If you're successful, don't crow. If you fail, don't croak."

When Dennis Holley of St. Louis held up a liquor store, he managed everything perfectly -- except for one tiny detail.

He pulled the robbery off without effort. He had the getaway car outside running and ready to go. He locked the car door so that no one could steal it while he was inside.

He really should have given a bit more thought, though, to how he was going to get into his locked car if his keys were in the ignition!

Fortunately for him, however, police flooded to the scene so that Holley could explain his problem. ∽ *The Associated Press*, August 29, 1990.

How come the only two cars going under the speed limit anywhere on the Interstate are doing it side-by-side ahead of you?

House speaker Tip O'Neill was describing what it was like being the leader of the Democratic opposition during the first years of the Reagan presidency. In his memoirs he said that he felt "like the guy in the old joke who gets hit by a steam-roller. Somebody runs to tell his wife about the accident.

"'I'm taking a bath right now,' she says. 'Could you just slip him under the door?'"

The test pilot realized he was in trouble. The plane was not responding the way it should be responding. He began looking around for the list of seven steps required to abandon the craft. The first step read: "Jettison the canopy". The pilot did just that. Where were the next six steps listed? You guessed it--on the roof of the canopy.

LOVE

Recently I read a love letter that one young lady wrote to her former fiance: Dear Jimmy--No words could ever express the great unhappiness I've felt since breaking our engagement. Please say you'll take me back. No one could ever take your place in my heart, so please forgive me. I love you, I love you, I love you! Yours forever, Marie. P.S. And congratulations on winning the state lottery. ☞ *Funny, Funny World*

I love the way John Sullivan, pastor of the Broadmoor Baptist Church in Shreveport, Louisiana, put it. Speaking of his first date with his wife he said, "I used my best charm. Before long I got the courage to blurt out to her, 'Let's go out tomorrow night.' She accepted right on the spot. It was my intent to kiss her on the first date but she said no. But friends, *SHE COULD HARDLY WAIT FOR THE SECOND DATE TO ROLL AROUND.*"

Dr. Peter Rhea Jones tells the story about a trapper who lived in the woods. He had his wife out there in the far wilderness and they had a little baby son. After the child was born, unfortunately, the wife abandoned her son and her husband and left them out in the wilderness and returned to life in a more civilized setting. The father and the son continued to live out in the far wilderness. They never went into town. Because of his wife's betrayal, the man became increasingly bitter toward women. He never told his boy about the opposite sex and the boy never saw any girls. Finally at age twenty the necessity came for them to travel some distance to a city to buy some goods. As they were coming into the city the boy began to notice something he had never seen before--all those pretty girls. And he said, "Pa, what are those?" His father, who was hostile toward women, said, "Aw, son, they're just silly gooses."

They went on doing their work and buying their supplies. When they were ready to go back home, the father generously said, "Son, we're going to go back and won't be returning for a long time. I'll buy you anything you want." The boy said definitely, "Pa, how 'bout one of them gooses?"

We know how the fellow felt who confided to his old friend that life was now empty because the woman he loved had refused to marry him.

"Don't let that get you down," said the friend. "A woman's 'no' often means 'yes'."

"She didn't say 'no'," came the dejected reply. "She said 'phooey'."

Several years ago there was a famous *PEANUTS* cartoon in which Shroeder, that piano-loving intellectual, was interrupted as he often was by his infatuated admirer, Lucy. Lucy asked Shroeder, "Shroeder, do you know what love is?" Shroeder abruptly stopped his playing, stood to his feet and said precisely, "Love: noun, to be fond of, a strong affection for or an attachment or devotion to a person or persons." Then he sat back down and resumed playing his piano. Lucy sat there stunned and then murmured sarcastically, "On paper, he's great."

A young man was trying to convince his sweetheart to marry him. She continued to resist. Finally he said, "Honey, is there anyone else?" She replied in a tone of desperation, "There must be."

A young soldier who was stationed overseas was writing to his girlfriend. He decided to send her a telegram because he thought that would make more of an impression. So he gave the telegraph operator a message to send: "I love you. I love you. I love you. John."

The telegraph operator said, "Son, for the same amount of money you can send one more word."

So he amended his message to read like this: "I love you. I love you. I love you. Cordially, John."

A young man entered a jewelry store and handed the jeweler a ring, stammering that he wished it marked with some names.

The jeweler was sympathetic. "What names do you wish it marked with?" he asked.

"'From Jim to Sarah,'" the young man whispered, red-faced.

The jeweler looked from the ring to the young man and smiled. "Take my advice, young fellow," he said. "Have it engraved simply, 'From Jim.'"

An Eskimo said to his girlfriend, "I would drive my dogs a thousand miles to say, 'I love you.'"

She responded, "That's a lost of mush!"

Daughter: "I'm sure he's the one for me. When he holds me close I can hear his heart pounding."

Mom: "Yeah? Well, your daddy fooled me that way for a whole year by wearing a cheap dollar watch."

Note this announcement given in chapel at a very conservative church college: "Students should observe that there is one legitimate exception to the rule concerning no physical contact of any kind between men and women students. If a male student happens to see a female student about to fall to the ground, it is permissible to touch her to break her fall. However, we shall not tolerate any young woman making a practice of falling."

Love is like a steam radiator -- it keeps you warm even though its 90 percent hot air. ∞ Judy Casanova

A young man was talking to his buddy about his new girlfriend. He said, "Since I met her I can't eat, drink, or sleep."
"Why's that?" asked his buddy.
"Because," he said, "I'm broke."

A couple were working together in a factory when the lights went out. When the lights came on again the young lady said, "Frank, you shouldn't have done that."
"Shouldn't have done what?"
"You shouldn't have kissed me when the lights went out."
"I didn't kiss you when the lights went out." He looked around belligerently at the people filing out. "But I'd like to catch the fellow who did. I'd teach him."
"Oh, Frank, you couldn't teach him anything."

Two buddies were talking about their girlfriends, and one commented to the other that he had changed his lifestyle a great deal to please his girlfriend. "You stopped smoking because she asked you to?"
"Yes," answered the man. "I quit drinking, cursing, and gambling, too."
His friend looked at him incredulously and asked, "Then why didn't you marry her?"
"Because after all that changing I found I could do better!"

There was the case of the chorus girl who swept into the dressing room with a mink coat draped casually over her arm. "Dearie," asked one of the girls, "how did you ever get such a gorgeous mink? Why, I've been struggling for years to get one."
"Honey," replied the other, "you mustn't struggle--ever."

An aggressive fellow: "I am a man of few words. Will you let me kiss you or won't you?"

Replied the demure miss: "Usually, I would not. But you have talked me into it."

He: "You know anybody who wants to buy a love seat? I've got one for sale."

She: "Does it work?"

As one wag has put it, love is a ticklish sensation around the heart that can't be scratched.

A young man, after weeks of agonizing, finally summoned up enough courage to ask the girl's father for his daughter's hand in marriage.

"I'll have to think about that for a while," the father said gruffly. "And I'm sure I needn't remind you that whoever marries my daughter gets a rare and beautiful prize."

"Oh, really?" exclaimed the fellow, relaxing a bit. "What are my chances of seeing it now?"

Two Junior High girls were walking home from school. Greg was on the other side of the street. One nudged the other excitedly, "There's Greg!" The other replied, "Oh, we're not speaking any more. I've lost all interest in him. We haven't spoken for 3 days, 6 hours, and 23 minutes."

A card-and-gift shop received a call from a young woman who had ordered wedding invitations just two weeks before. She wanted to know if it was too late to make a few changes on them. They told her to give them the new information and they would check with the printer.

"Okay," she said. "It's a different date, a different church and a different guy."

A young man had been sick for a while and finally went to the doctor for a remedy. The doctor said he just needed a little more diversion from his high pressure job, and suggested he try dating some girls. Several months later the man returned to the doctor. "Well," asked the doctor, "did my advice work?" "Sure," said the patient, "but I came back to ask you if you could recommend something to get my mind back on my job."

A farm boy and a pretty girl were walking down the road one evening. In one hand the boy carried a cane, in the other a chicken, he had a pail on his back and was leading a goat. Soon they came to a long dark lane.

The girl held back and said, "I'm afraid to walk through there with you because you might try to kiss me."

The boy looked at her and said, "How in the world could I do that with all the stuff I'm carrying?"

"Well, you might stick the cane in the ground, tie the goat to it, and put the chicken under the pail."

Dear Abby: I'm 19 years old and not very experienced, but my mother told me to be careful of men with moustaches. Is there any truth in this?

Dear Anita: Yes...and also be careful of men without them.

In the cartoon *MOMMA*, the daughter enters the room holding hands with a young man and says, "Momma, you're looking at two young people very much in love." A grin spreads across Momma's face until her daughter adds, "Jack here is in love with Bernice, and I'm in love with Stan."

The witty Oliver Herford has defined a kiss as, "A course of procedure, cunningly devised, for the mutual stoppage of speech at a moment when words are superfluous."

Adalai Stevenson once told a story about a young man who approached the father of his beloved to ask approval for their joining in matrimony. The father was skeptical. "I doubt very much," he said, "that you will ever be able to support my daughter. I can barely manage it myself." The young man thought for a moment and replied, "Sir, I believe I have it. You and I could just pool our resources."

There is a humorous little story that came out of Hollywood many years ago. A handsome, famous movie star checked into a hospital. As might be expected, every nurse in the hospital was very attentive to his needs. One particularly attractive nurse was at his side nearly every time he moved. When he finally indicated that he would like to be alone for a little while she said, "Now if you want anything at all you need only to pull this cord." The movie star gave his irresistible smile and said, "Thank you, my dear, but what is the cord attached to?" She smiled back and answered, "Me."

LUCK

I read about a man in Memphis who opened his car trunk one day and discovered a dusty package inside. He had bought a wastebasket for his wife as a Christmas gift, but had forgotten to give it to her. Sheepishly he took the package home and presented it to his spouse. When she saw it, she burst into tears of joy. It was their wedding anniversary and she was afraid he had forgotten.

Did you hear about the young man who was caught carrying a bomb on an airplane? When confronted, he claimed that he always carried a bomb with him on airplanes. After all, he asked, what are the odds against there ever being two bombs on the same plane?

In 1972 a Czechoslovakian woman named Vera Czermak was so upset by the news her husband had betrayed her that she tried to commit suicide by leaping from a third-story window. She jumped and landed on her husband, killing him.

Comedian Bob Hope was at the airport recently to meet his wife, Dolores, who was flying in after doing some charity work for the Catholic Church. When her private plane pulled in, they put the steps down. The first two people off the plane were Catholic priests, then came Dolores, and then came four more Catholic priests. Hope nudged a friend and said, "I don't know why she just doesn't buy insurance like everybody else."

"George, you've been losing and finding that ball all day. First in the woods, then under the rocks. Now it's lost somewhere in the swamp. C'mon, give it up!"
"I can't."
"Why not?"
"It's my lucky ball."

No matter what happened to a certain gold miner he always described it as pure luck. It was a particularly bitter winter. He was nearly freezing to death, but he kept digging for gold in the granite-like ground. Finally, as the earth thawed in the Spring and he was down to his last meager ration of food, he broke through the hard crust and dug and dug until at last he hit a box. Inside the box was a carton of canned food left behind by some earlier miner. "Boy am I lucky!" he said. "It could have been gold."

MARRIAGE

In a newspaper cartoon recently a woman with folded arms and a superior expression on her face says to her husband, "A good husband needs to be strong, caring and sensitive. You have all but three of those qualities."

There was an Alan Alda movie a few years back entitled "Four Seasons." It is about three couples who have been friends for years and have always vacationed together. They followed this routine for twenty consecutive summers. Before the twenty-first vacation, however, one of the couples divorces. The husband remarries and on the next vacation brings his new wife. This causes all kinds of discomfort. Finally the husband is confronted by a furious Carol Burnett, who plays one of the other wives. She tells him how disgusted she is with him over the divorce and finally says with fury, "Why didn't you just stay in there and fight it out like the rest of us?"

You may have heard about a new bride who was a bit embarrassed to be known as a honeymooner. So when she and her husband pulled up to the hotel, she asked him if there was any way that they could make it appear that they had been married a long time. He responded, "Sure. You carry the suitcases!"

We all know former president Jimmy Carter's commitment to marriage. Frank S. Mead tells about a memo Carter is said to have sent to his aides suggesting that any who were "living in sin" should become formally attached. Even he, however, had some fun with the wedding vows. When his former speech writer, Rick Hertzberg, married Michele Slung, Mr. Carter edited the vows in the marriage service as if it were a speech Hertzberg had written. For example, Carter circled, "till death do us part" and wrote, "Too morbid--do you want to alienate every sick person in America?" When he got to, "I, Rick, take you, Michele, to be my lawful wedded wife," the former President deleted "wife" and inserted "partner," warning, "Do not use sexist expressions." Next to "For better, for worse, for richer, for poorer," Carter wrote, "polarizing--how about the middle ground?"

One young adult put it this way: "A wedding is a funeral where you smell your own flowers."

There is a familiar cartoon about an elderly couple on a Sunday afternoon drive in their car. They are driving behind a cuddling young couple who are more interested in each other than they are in the road in front of them. The little old lady looks across at her husband behind the wheel of the car, then looks at the two young people in front of them, and asks her husband, "Why don't we sit together like that anymore?" Quick as a flash the old man answers, "Well, dear, I haven't moved."

An obvious example of "Doormat" was Jean Stapleton's marvelously played Edith Bunker on "All in the Family." In one scene Edith is talking to her friend Amelia. The dialogue went something like this:
Amelia: "Of all the people I know, you're practically the only one who has a happy marriage."
Edith: "Really? Me and Archie ... Oh, thank you."
Amelia: "What is your secret, Edith?"
Edith: "Oh, I ain't got no secret. Archie and me still have our fights. Of course, we don't let them go on too long. Some-body always says 'I'm sorry.' And Archie always says, 'It's okay, Edith.'" ∞ Spencer Marsh, *Edith the Good*, (New York: Harper & Row, 1977).

A want ad appeared in the newspapers sometime back: "For sale: One 52-year old husband. Never remembers an-niversaries, birthdays, or special days. Seldom holds hands, hugs, kisses, or says, 'I love you.' Rarely is kind or tender. Will sell cheap--two cents. Call 555-0366. Will dicker."

Heinrich Heine left this clause in his will: "I leave my en-tire estate to my wife on the condition that she remarry; then there will be at least one man to regret my death."

One man inscribed on his wife's tombstone :

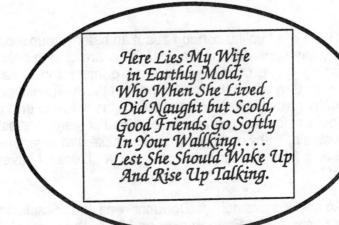

Here Lies My Wife
in Earthly Mold;
Who When She Lived
Did Naught but Scold,
Good Friends Go Softly
In Your Walking. . . .
Lest She Should Wake Up
And Rise Up Talking.

A woman attended a wedding with her 24-year-old bachelor son. He appeared unaffected by the ceremony until the bride and groom lighted a single candle with their candles and then blew out their own. With that he brightened and whispered, "I've never seen that done before."

His mother whispered back, "You know what it means, don't you?" His response: "No more old flames?"

Another woman sought the advice of a fortune-teller, who said, "Prepare yourself for widowhood. Your husband is about to die a violent death."

The wife sighed deeply and asked, "Will I be acquitted?"

In a wedding ceremony I heard about, the minister said, "Wilt thou..." and the groom wilted!

Archie Bunker says to Gloria: "Me and your mother think the same. And I know, 'cause I do her thinking for her."

On his fiftieth wedding anniversary an old gentleman gave his recipe for marital happiness:

"I've always tried to treat Ma in such a fashion that if I died, it would take more than a hot water bottle to replace me."

A female voice came over the telephone: "Is this the Fidelity Insurance Company?" "Yes, Ma'am," the receptionist replied. "Can I help you?" The caller continued, "I want to talk with someone about having my husband's fidelity insured."

Dr. Paul Popenoe, the famous marriage counselor, was talking to a young husband who had been openly critical of his wife. Dr. Popenoe was explaining how two become one in marriage. In a smart reply the husband said, "Yes, but which one?"

Four men asked a fifth to join them for a game of cards. He declined, saying he had to go home to his wife.

"Are you a man," asked one friend, "or a mouse?"

"I am a man," said the reluctant one, "Martha's afraid of mice."

A mother quizzed her grown daughter on her current boyfriend. "Just what kind of man are you interested in?" she finally asked. The daughter pointed to her father and said, "Like him--with a few minor modifications." Her father grinned triumphantly. "It's taken me thirty years to modify that one," her mother responded. "It doesn't come in a twenty-six-year-old model!"

A few years ago, someone wrote to Abigail Van Buren: "Dear Abby, I'm single; I'm forty years old; I'd like to meet a man about the same age who has no bad habits." Abby replied, "So would I!"

Two single women were talking. One said she was so desperate for a husband that she ran an ad in the "Personals" column of the newspaper advertising for a husband. She was discouraged, though. All the replies she got were from wives offering her their husbands.

A family counselor once said that what most wives want is a man they can look up to, but not one that will look down on them.

One husband knew that every year on the family's way to their vacation spot, just as they would get about eighty miles out of town, his wife would cry out, "Oh, no! I'm sure I left the iron on." Each year they would return home only to find it unplugged. One year, however, was different; the man had anticipated what was coming. When his wife gasped, "We must go back, I just know I left the iron on," he stopped the car, reached under his seat, and handed his wife the iron. ᗧAllen Klein, *The Healing Power of Humor,* (Los Angeles, California: Jerry Tarcher, Inc., 1989).

When I first met my wife, she was a schoolteacher. I used to write her passionate love letters--and she'd send them back corrected. I must be the only man in the world who returned from his honeymoon and received a report card. It said, "Dick is neat and friendly and shows a keen interest in fun and games." ᗧ Dick Lord, comedian

Counselor: "What first attracted you to this woman?"
Bachelor: "Her forthrightness, straightforwardness and frankness."
Counselor: "Why then are you now telling me you want to end the relationship?"
Bachelor: "Her forthrightness, straightforwardness and frankness." ᗧ Roger Dunnette in *Land O' Lakes Mirror*

In *MOTLEY'S CREW*, Motley is reading a little book entitled "Vows." "For better, for worse, for richer, for poorer, in sickness and in health."

He closes the book, smiles and says to his wife, "Sorry, Mabel. There's not a word in here about one spouse helping the other spouse fix up the house."

As Mabel drags him off to a home improvement center, Motley, says, "Maybe, this is the 'for better or for worse.'"

The next time you doubt your wife's judgment, stop and look at who she married. ∞ Herm Albright

You don't have to be smutty to enjoy some forms of sexual humor. One story that tickles me is about the pastor who got his "tang tongled." He meant to pronounce the couple "lawfully joined together." That's not what came out, though. What he said was, "I now pronounce this couple joyfully loined together." I hope that is how it is between you and your spouse. I hope you are joyfully loined together.

A woman, married to a wealthy Texan, said, "I didn't want to marry him for his money, but how else was I going to get it?"

Many a woman's last-minute shopping race for a gift for her husband ends up in a tie.

There is a story about a near-sighted pastor. Someone passed him a note. The note read like this: "John Jones, having gone to sea, his wife desires prayers from the congregation for his safety." But as the near-sighted pastor read the note, he misplaced a comma and the sentence came out like this: "John Jones, having gone to see his wife, desires prayers from the congregation for his safety."

There is a classic story of the woman who hired a medium to bring back the spirit of her dead husband. When he appeared in a ghostly form, she asked, "Honey, is it really better up there?" Without hesitation he answered, "Oh, yes, it is much better. But I'm not up there!"

Midwest newspaper ad: Idaho bachelor wants wife. Must be interested in farming and own tractor. Please enclose picture, of tractor.

MEDICINE

A hypochondriac told his doctor in great alarm that he was sure he had a fatal liver disease.

"Nonsense!" protested the doctor. "You would never know it if you had that disease. With that ailment there's no discomfort of any kind."

"I know," gasped the patient. "My symptoms exactly."

An elderly woman walked in and said, "Doctor, you probably don't remember me. But ten years ago you told me to go home, go to bed and stay there till you called back. But you never called." The doctor replied, "Didn't I? Well, what're you doing out of bed?"

I love the story of the man who was told by his doctor, "I'm sure I have the answer to your problem."

The man answered, "I certainly hope so, doctor. I should have come to you long ago."

The doctor asked, "Where did you go before?"

"I went to the pharmacist."

The doctor snidely remarked, "What kind of foolish advice did he give you?"

"He told me to come to see you!"

A lady in the waiting room was complaining bitterly about having to wait so long for the doctor. Seems he took so much time with some patients that he was always behind schedule.

"Why don't you change doctors?" another patient asked,

"Because," the complainer admitted, "I'm one of the patients he takes so much time with." ∞ Ivern Hall in *Quote*

The psychiatrist asked what the patient had dreamed the previous night. "I didn't dream at all," replied the patient.

"How do you expect me to help you," chided the doctor, "if you don't do your homework."

A psychiatrist was awakened in the dead of night by one of his patients, a kleptomaniac, who blurted into the phone: "Doctor, I've got this urge to steal real bad."

Psychiatrist: "For heaven's sake! It's 2 a.m.! Just take two ashtrays and call me in the morning."

When a bus load of people entered a large cafeteria, the group leader approached the manager. "Sir, I'm Mr. Harris of the Halfway House. These nice folks are former mental patients. They've all been cured, but they do have one small idiosyncrasy: they'll want to pay you in bottle tops. Now if you'll be so kind as to humor them in this way, I'll take care of the bill when they're through."

The manager, wanting to be a good citizen, went along and collected the bottle tops. The group's leader returned, and with gratitude said, "Thank you so much. I'll pay the bill now. Do you have change for a garbage can lid?"
∞ Don Emmitte

Somewhere I heard about identical twin brothers who lived in the same town where one was a physician and the other was a pastor. One Monday morning, the doctor ran into someone who said, "That was a marvelous sermon you preached last Sunday." "Oh, no," the doctor protested, "you've got the wrong man. That was my brother. He preaches and I practice."

A man was choking on a bone. Immediately he called for a doctor who removed it. The victim asked, "So what do I owe you?" Replied the doctor, "How about the amount you were ready to pay while the bone was still in your throat?"

One comedian says he's figured out what doctors scribble on those prescriptions: "I've got my 50 bucks, now you get yours."

A man died recently and was touring Heaven, his new home. He thought he would grab a bite at the celestial cafeteria. He was standing patiently in line when all of a sudden, from around a corner comes a man in a white jacket who jumped in front of the first person in line. The man was mortified. "I can't believe anybody would act that way in Heaven," he said to a new friend later in the day. "Was he wearing a white jacket?" asked his friend. "Yes," replied the man. "Did he have a stethoscope in his pocket?" "Come to think about it," said the man, "he did have a stethoscope in his pocket." "Oh," chuckled his friend, "don't let that bother you. That was God. He loves to play doctor."

A patient limped into the doctor's office. The doctor handed the patient a large pill. Momentarily the doctor was distracted by a noise outside the room. Meanwhile the patient limped over to the sink and choked down the pill. Then the doctor returned with a bucket and said, "Now drop the pill in the bucket and we'll soak your foot."

Someone has defined a specialist as a doctor with a smaller practice but a bigger yacht.

MEMORY

A man was sitting at the breakfast table reading his newspaper when his wife breezed through the kitchen, gave him a light kiss on the cheek and said matter-of-factly, "I'll bet you've forgotten what day this is." The husband answered defensively, "I have not!" He went back to reading the paper while she rushed upstairs to finish getting ready.

All the way to work it bugged him, "What day is this?" He knew she was very sensitive about his forgetting Valentine's Day, anniversaries, etc. But for the life of him he could not think what day this was. He decided he better not take any chances. Driving home he stopped and purchased a box of candy, a dozen roses and a gift-wrapped bottle of her favorite perfume. Opening the door he rushed back into the kitchen where she was preparing the evening meal. "Surprise!" he said. She replied, "Oh, Sweetheart. This is the best Groundhog's Day I've ever had."

STUDIO ONE was one of the most popular shows in the golden days of live television. During one memorable broadcast, the scene was the interior of an airplane cabin. The scene called for the plane to be at an altitude of 30,000 feet, flying over the mountains of Tibet. Three men were in the cabin talking, when suddenly there was silence. One of the actors had forgotten his lines. Being a live production, of course, there were no retakes, no stopping of the action. That was it. Millions of eager viewers were glued to their black-and-white screens, waiting to see what would happen next. What did the actor do? He got to his feet, in an airplane cabin supposedly 30,000 feet over the mountains of Tibet, and voiced this immortal line: "Well, here's where I get off." He left the set and walked into history.

Modern Society

Dan Dailey in the *NEW YORK DAILEY NEWS* tells about overhearing a woman in New York who lived in an area near SoHo and NoHo. Because of the trouble in her own area, she calls it "UhOh".

Perhaps you would agree with Ogden Nash: "Progress was once a very good idea; however, it has been going on far too long."

As humorist Robert Orben says, "You have to question any period in history in which people are saying that God is dead and Elvis is alive."

Will Durant, the great historian, said, "When people ask me to compare the twentieth century to older civilizations, I always say the same thing: 'The situation is normal.'"

Woody Allen says modern man has no peace of mind, he finds himself in the midst of a crisis of faith. He is what we fashionably call 'alienated.' He has seen the ravages of war, he has known natural catastrophes, he has been to singles bars.

Most women can sympathize with Edith Bunker of television's *ALL IN THE FAMILY*. Son-in-law Mike asks, "Did you go to the women's meeting today?"
Edith answers, "Oh, no! With all the shopping, washing, and housecleaning, I didn't have time to be liberated today."

You can live on bland food so as to avoid an ulcer; drink no tea or coffee or other stimulants, in the name of health; go to bed early and stay away from night life; avoid all controversial subjects so as never to give offense; mind your own business and avoid involvement in other people's problems; spend money only on necessities and save all you can. But you can still break your neck in the bathtub, and it will serve you right. ∞ Eileen Guder, *God, But I'm Bored*

Where would Christianity be if Jesus got eight to ten years with time off for good behavior? ∞ N.Y. State Sen. James H. Donovan, arguing for capital punishment

In the cartoon *MOTLEY'S CREW,* Earl is awakened by the radio newscast: "Gang violence erupts into a bloody brawl...A freeway sniper is on the loose...and a psychopathic killer escapes from jail." Without moving, eyes still closed, Earl thinks: "Only Rambo would get up this morning."

A recent cartoon depicted an overturned Suzuki Samurai with a "For Sale or Trade" sign on it. A prospective buyer, hoping to negotiate a deal, was offering a Honda three wheeler, two pit bulldogs, and a set of lawn darts for a trade. ∞"Perspectives", *Newsweek*, June 20, 1988.

Charlie Brown in *PEANUTS* drags his bean bag chair in front of the television and turns the TV on.
Announcer: "Boy, have we got bad news for you tonight."
Charlie Brown: "How bad is it?'
Announcer: "We're not even going to give you the details at eleven!"

"I'm 100 percent in favor of progress," said a man, reacting badly to the threats he perceived around him. "It's all this change I'm against!"

The horse would have a good laugh these days if it could see all these motorists adjusting their shoulder harnesses.
The Milwaukee Journal

Last summer we drove our 1915 Ford Model T to an antique automobile show in a neighboring town. When we arrived, I was told that a business client wanted me to visit him at his nearby farm.

Late that day we set out. Unfamiliar with the roads, I stopped my vintage automobile, got out and walked up to a local resident who was mowing his lawn.

"I believe I'm a little lost," I began.

The man looked from me to the Model T. "You certainly are, mister," he agreed. "This is 1986!" John Gottschalk in *Reader's Digest*

We are like the man who went to the top of an 30-story building, jumped off, and as he passed the 20th story was heard to say, "So far so good."

An elderly doctor listened to the wails of a woman who bemoaned the disappearance of the family physician, the "good old-fashioned doctor." Finally he lost patience and replied, "Madam, if you will show me an old-fashioned family, I will produce a doctor for it." *Today's Health*

Do the little things in life make you happy? In an informal survey, California economist Harry Biederman asked almost 400 people exactly what those little things were. They said:

Having the elevator to my office go nonstop to the right floor.

Having my date unlock the door on my side after I help her into the car.

Having the rare experience of driving home from work and not being irritated by other drivers.

Seeing my children after work and having them pounce on me....

Not surprisingly, family life makes most people the happiest. Sex, on the other hand, came up dead last on the list. Doesn't sex make people happy? Yes, it probably does, says Biederman. But it's of such an intimate nature that people don't discuss it readily. "If a checklist had been provided for the survey, I'm sure sex would have ranked near the top," he says. ∞ *Psychology Today*

Patrick Henry shouted: "Give me liberty or give me death."
The next generation shouted: "Give me liberty."
Our generation shouts: "Give me." ∞ Source Unknown

Someone participating in a national poll was recently asked, "What do you think about cyclamates?" Her response was, "I think any two cyclamates who live together should get married."

Sometime back a cartoon showed the earth following a nuclear war. Only half of the sphere remains and a huge dark mushroom cloud looms above it. Over the ruins is the bearded and robed figure of God.

The caption read: "Well, there's six days' work shot."

Someone put it like this: "Grandfather owned a farm. Father owned a garden. Son owns a can opener."

A Girl Scout leader advised her Brownies: "Remember, girls, if you're lost in the woods at night, get your bearings from the sky. A glow will indicate the nearest shopping center."

The newspapers carried an intriguing story recently about a protest movement by students from Cabrillo College in Santa Cruz, CA. Like many movements that emanate from California, this was a crusade with a difference. The protesting students carried blank signs and blank leaflets. Bryan Finch, who organized the protest, said that protests have become so common that no one reads the signs or the leaflets anyway. His group was protesting the meaninglessness of most protests.

In 1910 Olav Olavson, a Swedish citizen, fell upon hard times and decided to sell his body for medical research after his death to the Karolinska Institute in Stockholm. The following year he inherited a fortune and resolved to buy himself back. The institute refused to sell its rights to his body, went to court, and won possession of it. Moreover, the institute obtained damages, since Olav had had two teeth pulled out without asking their permission as ultimate owner of his body. ∞ David Frost, *Book of the World's Worst Decisions,* (New York: Prince Paperbacks-Crown Publishers, Inc., 1983).

Recently, while shopping in a book store, I saw two signs which most of us understand all too well. One said, "The hurrier I go, the behinder I get!" And the other said, "I'm so far behind that if anything else were to happen, it would be two weeks before I could worry about it."

I never expected to see the day when girls would get sunburned in the places they do now. ∞ Will Rogers

A man on an ocean cruise fell overboard. He was floundering in the water, shouting and waving and trying to get the attention of those on board. Finally a lawyer spotted him and shouted, "Shall I prepare a suit against the cruise line in your behalf?" A politician saw him and promised that he would press a bill in congress next term to make sailing safer. Finally an evangelist saw him and said with a smile, "Yes, brother I see your hand, now, do I see another?"

There is that old story from centuries ago about three men in a boat, none of whom could swim. When they got out to the middle of the lake one of them took out an augur and began boring a hole in the bottom of the boat. The other two shouted, "What are you doing?"

"Mind your own business," said the one with the augur. "I'm drilling this hole beneath my seat alone. It has nothing to do with you."

"But," shouted the other two men, "we are all in the same boat!"

MONEY

A man of some wealth overheard a lady remarking, "Oh, if I only had fifty dollars I would be perfectly content."

He thought about that for a few moments. If the lady only had fifty dollars she would be content. He thought to himself, "Well, I can help her out." So he walked up to her and handed her a fifty dollar bill with his best wishes. She was very overt in her show of gratitude. She really appreciated his gift. As she walked away he heard her mumble under her breath, "Why on earth didn't I say one hundred dollars?"

A wife came to the living room one day after having answered the front door. "There's a man at the door who wants to see you about a bill you owe," she told her husband. "What does he look like?" the husband inquired. "He looks like you'd better pay him," the wife declared.

Some persons are concerned about money almost to the point of desperation. A mail carrier tells of greeting a four-year-old boy who had planted himself firmly in front of his family's mailbox and would not budge. With his feet spread wide and his arms folded, he told the mail carrier firmly, "My mom says she can't *TAKE* any more bills."

As somebody said: "A nickle goes a long way nowadays. You can carry it around for days and not find anything you can buy with it."

"Inflation is creeping up," a young man said to his friend. "Yesterday I ordered a $25 steak in a restaurant and told them to put it on my Visa...and it fit."

Things aren't always what they seem. A million dollar house in Beverly Hills could be a $600,000 house with a $400,000 burglar alarm. ☞ *Funny, Funny World*

A millionaire died one day after he had bequeathed half a million to his church and another half a million to each of his relatives. At the cemetery, the preacher noticed that among the well-dressed mourners was a shabby stranger who cried as though his heart were breaking. "I noticed you crying," said the preacher. "Were you related to the deceased?" "No," the young man responded, "I wasn't related at all." "Then, why are you crying?" queried the preacher. The man replied, "I just told you--because I wasn't related."

A little girl saved up enough money to buy her father a present for Father's Day, but she had one concern. "I can't be going downtown every month to make payments," she said to her mother. "Is there a store where they'll let you pay the whole thing at once?"

Boswell once observed to Johnson that there was no instance of a beggar dying for want in the streets of Scotland, "I believe, sir, you are very right," says Johnson, "but this does not arise from the want of beggars, but the impossibility of starving a Scotsman."

A certain clothing manufacturer turned out thousands of sweatshirts with "Money isn't everything" printed on them. He went bankrupt.

A lot of people believe that a millionaire's money is, to quote Mark Twain, twice tainted - "tain't yours" and "tain't mine."

During the Great Depression, Bernard Baruch accumulated billions of dollars.

A reporter once asked him, "Mr. Baruch, I know you're a very wealthy man. How much is going to be enough?"

He said, "Just a little more."

An old Jewish story tells about a beggar who went to the house of the wealthiest but most miserly man in town. "Sir," he said to the old skinflint, "I have sought charity from you before but never have you parted with so much as a penny. This time, however, my need is more serious than at any previous time. My family is hungry. We don't have much time."

This pathetic appeal failed to move the rich miser. He argued fiercely with the caller and then ordered him out of the house.

"Very well, I'll leave," said the beggar, "but first let me recite a short parable."

"Go ahead and recite it, but you won't get a cent!" grumbled the wealthy but stingy old man.

"Ever since the beginning of time," said the beggar, "no one has ever figured out why a dog grabs a pig by the ear when he catches it. According to the Talmud there is no man as poor as a dog nor is there any man as rich as a pig. So it must be clear to you, sir, that the dog secretly whispers into the pig's ear, 'If you are so rich then why are you such a pig?'"

Pat Schwab of Seattle, Washington, strikes oil in 25 words or less. She notes that "For the past few years, my watch word has been: I came, I saw, I bought! Or, as they say in Latin, 'Veni, Vidi, *VISA*'!" ∞ *Laughing Matters*

The Scotchman sent an indignant letter to the editor of the newspaper. He said that if any more stories about stingy Scotchmen appeared in the columns, he was going to stop borrowing the paper.

Once I knew a Baptist, he had a pious look.
He had been totally immersed, except his pocketbook.
He put a nickel in the plate, and then with might and main
He'd sing, "When we sunder part, it gives me inward pain."
∞ Contributed by Wade Burton

One man was already in the waters of the baptismal pool when he realized he had his wallet in his back pocket. He started to take it out, then changed his mind. "Shucks," he told his pastor, "go ahead and baptise my wallet too."

Did you hear about the wealthy Dallas oilman who went on vacation to Hawaii? He went out to the beach one afternoon to discover that his wife had just been rescued from the surf, and was being revived by the lifeguards. "What are you doing?" he asked. The lifeguards replied, "We are giving her artificial respiration." "Artificial nothing," the oilman shouted, "Give her the real thing. We can afford it."

A state trooper found a Yuppie by the roadside next to a demolished car, crying, "My BMW! I've lost my BMW!"

The trooper says, "Never mind the car. You've lost your left arm!"

The Yuppie looks down, and cries, "My Rolex! I've lost my Rolex!" ⌘ *The Jokesmith*

In the movie, "Oh, God!" the idea was advanced that the reason God gave Adam and Eve no clothes to wear was because God knew that once they had clothes, they would want pockets. Once they had pockets, they would want money.

An American history teacher, lecturing the class on the Puritans, asked: "What sort of people were punished in the stocks?"

To which a small voice from the back of the room responded: "The small investor."

The young couples' Sunday school class was studying the story of Abraham and Sarah, who in their 90s were blessed with a child, Isaac.

"What lesson," the teacher asked, "do we learn from this story?"

A young mother blurted out, "They waited until they could afford it."

I like the story about Ralph the cab driver who had accumulated $100,000 and was going to retire. As was customary, the company gave him a farewell dinner. At the toast, Ralph said a few words.

"I owe my retirement in part to my thrifty habits," said Ralph. "Even more, I owe it to the good judgment of my wife. But still more, I owe it to my aunt who died and left me $95,000."

A Texas millionaire stipulated in his will that he be buried in his favorite possession: his $90,000 Rolls Royce. When the time came, two laborers were shoveling the last bit of dirt onto the now buried luxury car. One finally turned to the other and said, "Boy! That's living!"

As Yogi Berra is quoted as saying: "A nickle ain't worth a dime anymore."

Cecil Rhodes was an enormously wealthy man. One day a newspaperman said to him, "You must be very happy." Rhodes replied, "Happy?! No! I spent my life amassing a fortune only to find I have spent half of it on doctors to keep me out of the grave, and the other half on lawyers to keep me out of jail!"

Someone once said that the Presbyterians, being Scots, would rather have their debts forgiven than their trespasses any day!

This advertisement appeared in an issue of *CONNOISSEUR*. It was headed as "Demoralize Thy Neighbor:"
"It's one thing to trundle by in a Bentley, Jaguar, Mercedes, or the like. Everyone in your neighborhood has one of these.
"It's quite another thing to come in for a landing in your Lagonda. The Lagonda is an Ashton Martin, and Ashton Martin reflects your personal style: everyone knows that you have one, but not everyone knows exactly what it is. The Lagonda is, in fact, the automobile paradox.
"For example, when many cars are made largely by robots, the Lagonda is made entirely by hand. The aluminum body panels are hammered into shape, welded, sanded, and finished with 23 coats of lacquer. (It has been said that looking into the finish of a Lagonda is like falling into a pool.) Even

the engine is hand-made and signed by one of the four engine builders.

"The paradox continues.

"The Lagonda is powerful and safe. Should you wish to drive one-fifth the speed of sound, this is the safest car in the world to do it in.

"For all its power, handling capacity, and advanced electronics instrumentation, the Lagonda is remarkably reliable and essentially a simple car. We build a Lagonda at a rate of three a week. Twenty-four are designated for the United States market each year. That is about as fast and as many as we can manage.

"Should your neighbors ask you, as you glide by, what kind of car the Lagonda is, by all means tell them. Should they ask you where they can get one, tell them they probably can't. That should do it."

Billionaire Jean Paul Getty was once asked the secret of his success. Said Getty, "Some people find oil. Others don't."

MORALITY

Lloyd Ogilvie tells about a good friend, Johnny Grant, a popular television and radio host who is also an outstanding community leader and a committed Christian. Johnny Grant used a one-liner that Ogilvie says is worth remembering. Many of you remember a popular movie of a year or so ago entitled, "Children of a Lesser God." Johnny Grant said that the problem today is that too many Christians want to be "children of a looser God."   ∽Lloyd Olgivie, *12 Steps to Living Without Fear(Waco: Word Books, 1987)*

Psychiatrist Karl Menninger in his famous book *WHATEVER BECAME OF SIN?* (New York: Hawthorn

Books, 1973) notes that American Presidents used to mention sin once in awhile, but that none has done so since 1953.

The Republicans refer to the problems of "pride" and "self-righteousness." The Democrats refer to "shortcomings." But none use the grand old sweeping concept of sin anymore. Thus, it seems, we as a nation stopped sinning thirty-five years ago! And, speaking of politics: a poll on Heaven and Hell in the Des Moines Register awhile back found that only one Republican in 35 expects to end up in Hell, whereas one Democrat in nine assumes he will. I am not sure what that means. It may mean that it does little good to preach hellfire and brimstone to a congregation that is filled with people who don't believe there is a chance in hell that they will end up there. ☞ Dr. Donald Strobe

As somebody has said, "Even Mason and Dixon had to draw the line somewhere."

Ancient myths tell about Diogenes who took up his lamp in search of an honest man. Someone said that when he got to New York somebody stole his lamp.

I read recently a humorous list of persons who were convinced that their sins were hidden:

The thief was sure that the church was a safe hideout. Just inside he spied a rope hanging. Up he climbed, only to hear the church bell ringing his whereabouts.

A Mexico City man snatched a woman's purse and dashed into a doorway to hide. It turned out to be the door of a police station, where he was questioned and later identified by his victim.

It happened in New York: a man picked up an alarm clock and headed for the nearest exit. The clock, concealed under his coat, went off before he could get out of the store.

MOTHERS

William Jennings Bryan, back in 1892, was a freshman congressman. Bryan was famous for his silver-tongued oratory but one day he was stumped when a woman debated him. It was the first time anybody saw William Jennings Bryan speechless. He had been speaking that day on the Pilgrim fathers.

A lady named Mr. Henrietta Szold pointed a finger at William Jennings Bryan and said, "Mr. Bryan, have you nothing to say about the Pilgrim mothers?"

Bryan asked, "Why? What about them?"

She stood tall and said to William Jennings Bryan, "The Pilgrim mothers ought to be saluted. They not only had to endure the same things the Pilgrim fathers did; they had to endure the Pilgrim fathers as well."

I heard about one little boy and girl who saved up to buy their mother a Mother's Day bouquet. They went to the florist and came back with a wreath with a ribbon on it that said, *REST IN PEACE*. They thought it was appropriate. She always wanted a little peace and quiet so she could rest well. Obviously that was not the intent of the floral wreath, but it served it's purpose.

I appreciated the story of one mother with four small children at home. A friend gave her a play pen, and she wrote a thank you note. "I love it. I sit down in it in the middle of the living room. The children can't get to me for hours."

Quarreling between her two sons prompted one mother to rush to the kitchen. Eight-year-old Bobby and four-year-old Jackie were having a tug-of-war with the cookie jar. Only one cookie remained in the jar, and each boy thought it was his.

Taking the cookie jar from the two youngsters, the mother calmly announced, "I'll solve the problem for you. I'll eat the last cookie myself."

The boys looked up at their mother in unbelief. Then the four-year-old, with a mischievous grin on his face, said, "Oh, no you won't, Mommy. Whoever heard of a selfish mother?"

Many of you will identify with the mother whose 16-year-old daughter was horrified to see her mother on Mother's Day at the sink washing dishes. "Oh, Mom, you shouldn't have to do dishes on Mother's day." Clearly touched by this thoughtfulness, the mother began to take off her apron and give it to her daughter. The daughter added, "They'll keep until tomorrow."

DENNIS THE MENACE was talking to Margaret one day. "I wonder what my mom would like for Mother's day?" he asked.

Margaret answered, "Why don't you promise to go to bed when she tells you to, to keep you room cleaned up, to eat all your vegetables at dinner--even brush your teeth after eating, and wash you hands before."

Dennis looked at her, scowling thoughtfully. "No, I mean something practical."

MOTIVATION

One man asked his best friend why he did not go to work. "Are you afraid of work?" he wanted to know. "No," his friend answered, "I'm not afraid of work at all. In fact I can lay right down beside it and go to sleep."

Perhaps you've heard the story about the old drunk who was paid to sit-up all night in a funeral home in a viewing room with an open coffin in case anyone came late to pay their respects. Unknown to the town drunk, he was being set-up by some practical jokers. In the quietness of the early morning hours, the body in the coffin sat up and screamed. Very calmly the drunk got up, staggered over to the casket, and pushed the body back down saying, "If you're dead, lie down and act like it."

The story is told about a golfer who is repeatedly missing with a five-iron and hitting an ant hill. With every miss of the ball he slays another million or so ants. Getting a little frightened, one ant says to the other one, "We'd better get on the ball if we want to stay alive."

Many of you are familiar with country music star Mel Tillis. Mel's autobiography is entitled Stutterin' Boy, and it is well-named. Mel has always stuttered very badly, except when he sings. He tells about the time he and songwriter Wayne Walker were asleep in a motel on the ground floor. A friend of theirs named Johnny Paycheck, another country singer, needed Wayne's car keys. He didn't want to wake Mel and Wayne, so he crawled through the motel window and then tried to find Wayne's keys. Mel woke up about this time and saw someone fumbling around in the room but didn't know who it was. He tried to say something but his tongue and his vocal chords both froze up on him. No words came out, no matter how hard he tried to speak. Finally, in desperation, he SANG. That was the only way the words would come out. He sang, "Wayne, Wayne, we're being robbed."

Some people are motivated by a desperate situation. A famous paratrooper was speaking to a group of young recruits. When he had finished his prepared talk and called for questions, one young fellow raised his hand and said, "What made you decide to make your first jump?"

The paratrooper's answer was quick and to the point: "An airplane at 20,000 with three dead engines."

A letter was addressed to the General Electric Company from a little girl in the third grade who had chosen to investigate electricity for her class project. "I'm trying to get all the information I can," her letter said, "so please send me any booklets and papers you have. Also would it be asking too much for you to send me a little sample of electricity?"

It was both heroic and dramatic. The fire in a small warehouse had been burning for hours. The little community had no means of fighting it. Other buildings were being threatened. Suddenly down the hill roared an old truck. Right through the flames the truck sped, scattering farm workers who had been riding in back.

Jumping from the truck they beat at the flames with their coats until the fire was out. The grateful citizens of the town wanted to reward them. They raised over five hundred dollars. They presented it to the driver of the truck and asked him what he was going to do with the money. Without a moment's hesitation he replied, "You can be sure the first thing I'm gonna do is to fix the brakes on my truck."

NEW YEAR'S

From *FOR BETTER OR WORSE* comic: The family is sitting around the breakfast table and father says, "Well, here we are in a brand new year. I think we should all make some resolutions, don't you?"

MOTHER: "O.K. I resolve not to criticize, to nag less and to bake more often."

FAMILY RESPONSE: "Right on! Neat! Yeah!"

FATHER: "I resolve not to lose my temper, and to fix all the things in the house that need repairs."

FATHER: "I resolve not to lose my temper, and to fix all the things in the house that need repairs."

FAMILY RESPONSE: "Great! OK!!!"

ELIZABETH: "I resolve to brush Farley (the dog), to keep my room clean and not to fight with Michael."

RESPONSE: "Good!"

MICHAEL: "I resolve to play road hockey, hang out with my friends, and to watch more TV."

MOTHER: "Wait a minute! We all made real promises. Your resolutions are worthless."

MICHAEL: "I know...but at least mine will be kept!"

Wife to Spouse: "I don't want to brag, but here it is February and I've kept everyone of my New Year's resolutions. I've kept them in a manila folder in the back of my desk!"
☜ Robert Orben

One day Lucy and Linus had a chicken wishbone and were going to pull it to make a wish. Lucy was explaining to Linus that if he got the bigger half of it his wish would come true.

Linus said to her, "Do I have to say the wish out loud?"

Lucy said, "Of course, if you don't say it out loud it won't come true." So Lucy went ahead and made her wishes first. She said, "I wish for four new sweaters, a new bike, a new pair of skates, a new dress and one hundred dollars."

It came time for Linus to make his wishes, and he said, "I wish for a long life for all of my friends, I wish for world peace, I wish for great advancements in medical research."

About that time, Lucy took the wishbone and threw it away saying, "Linus, that's the trouble with you. You're always spoiling everything."

Some of us make resolutions like one man named George I heard about. He said to a friend: "There's nothing like getting up at six in the morning, going for a run around the park, and taking a brisk shower before breakfast."

His friend Bob asked, "How long have you been doing this?"

George: "I start tomorrow."

OPPORTUNITY

A widow in a certain retirement home was playing bridge with three other ladies. A man walked in--a new resident.

One of the ladies waved at him and spoke. "Hello! You're new here, aren't you?"

He replied, "Yes, I am. As a matter of fact I just moved in, and I was taking a little stroll around to look the place over."

Another lady asked, "Where did you move from?"

He replied, "Oh, I was just released after twenty years in San Quentin."

Surprised, one of the ladies asked, "San Quentin? What were you in for?"

He said, "Well, I murdered my wife."

Immediately this little widow lady perked up and said: "Oh, then you're single?..."

An angry reader once stormed into a newspaper office waving the current edition, asking to see the one who wrote the obituary column. He was referred to a cub reporter to whom he showed the column which included this man's own obituary. He said, "You see, I am very much alive. I demand an immediate retraction!" The reporter replied, "I never retract a story. But I tell you what I'll do. I'll put you in the birth column and give you a fresh start!"

Bishop Gerald Kennedy had just arrived in a city for a preaching engagement. Exhausted from travelling, he settled down in his hotel room to get some rest before the service. Just as he lay down, he heard, to his dismay, the sounds of a violin next door. He was just about to go next door and complain when the maid came to service his room and said, "Aren't you lucky! You get to hear Jascha Heifetz play and you don't even have to buy a ticket!"

ORGANIZATION

Often we forget what our main business is. A supersalesman sold a complicated filing system to a thriving business. Three months later, the salesman paid the company a visit. "How is the filing system working out?" "Magnificently," replied the manager. "Out of this world."

"How is business?" asked the salesman to the manager. The manager said, "We had to give up our business to run the filing system!"

Lucy once demanded that Linus change TV channels, threatening him with her fist if he didn't.

"What makes you think you can walk right in here and take over?" asks Linus.

"These five fingers," says Lucy. "Individually they're nothing but when I curl them together like this into a single unit, they form a weapon that is terrible to behold."

"Which channel do you want?" asks Linus sheepishly.

Turning away, he looks at his fingers and says, "Why can't you guys get organized like that?"

John Claypool tells a parable about a young man who was applying for a job. As a part of the application process, the young man had to take an aptitude test. He arrived at the appointed time, was given instructions about the test, and then was ushered into the testing room.

Immediately, though, the young man became enamored with the utensils at his disposal: he straightened the paper on the desk, sharpened his pencils and shined his chair. In fact, he became so engrossed in the material around him he never got around to taking the test! When time was up and the tests were collected, he had nothing to show for his efforts but a neat desk, finely sharpened pencils and an immaculate chair.

Needless to say, he didn't get the job. ∞ Judson Edwards, *Regaining Control of Your Life,* (Minneapolis: Bethany House Publishing, 1989).

The Marine Sergeant was trying to enforce the old rules of Marine discipline with a modern psychological idea that you should always explain why. He was heard yelling at a squadron of green recruits: "Take a look at yourselves! Shoes not shined properly, haircuts terrible, ties crooked, and whiskers like you haven't shaved in a week. *SUPPOSE SOME COUNTRY SUDDENLY DECLARED WAR ON US! WHAT WOULD WE DO?"*

PASTOR

We are like the six-year-old girl who said to her mother, "The number one problem in the United States is pollution. I read that in my *WEEKLY READER.* Everybody knows that the number one problem in the United States is pollution--everybody but our preacher. He thinks that it is sin. I think that's just because he's a preacher."

A small girl said to her preacher-father, "Daddy, is it true that your sermons are inspired by God?" The pastor modestly replied, "I hope so, dear." "Then why," asked his puzzled daughter, "do I see you erasing and changing things in them?"

A few years ago, when the late Dr. Jitsuo Morikawa was installed as pastor of First Baptist Church, our neighbor congregation next door, the local newspaper was supposed to announce "The Installation of Dr. Morikawa." It appeared in print as: "The '*INSULATION*' of Dr. Morikawa." I sent a copy of the fascinating typo to the Christian Century for Martin Marty's column, with the note saying, "I always thought Jitsuo was pretty much a live-wire...but I guess he's properly insulated now!" ∞ Dr. Donald Strobe

It seems that a preacher came across a character in the Gospels called "Simon the Leaper." He imagined all sorts of things that this Leaper character might have done--leaping from mountain to mountain, hill to hill. And he preached a sermon on it. Then someone brought it to his attention that the man's name was "Simon the Leper." To which the preacher replied, "I don't see the need to throw away a good sermon just because of a difference in pronunciation!"

A priest once said to Groucho Marx, "Oh, Mr. Marx, I want to thank you for bringing so much joy into the world." To which Groucho, always quick on the uptake, replied, rather ungraciously, "And I want to thank you for taking so much out."

The wife of an Episcopal priest was in the hospital for minor surgery. He decided to stop to see her as one of his regular hospital visits. There he stood chatting with her in his clerical collar. Then, he gave her a long passionate kiss and left the room. The lady in the next bed stared in disbelief, then said to the wife, "You know, I've been a faithful Methodist all my life, but my pastor doesn't treat me like that at all."

There is a time-honored story about a young minister preaching his first sermon in a tiny country church. He was so-o-o nervous. His nervousness showed as he tried to expound on this text. "The Master fed the multitude," he said, his voice quivering, "with 5,000 loaves and 2,000 fish."

An old fellow sitting on the front row chuckled sarcastically and said, "Why, I could do that."

The next Sunday the young pastor tried again. "Last Sunday I meant to say that the Master fed 5,000 people with five loaves and two tiny fish." Then he turned to the old man and asked, "Could you do that?"

The old fellow grinned and said, "I could if you'd let me use what we had left over last week."

PEACE

The comics often express what most of us are thinking and sometimes don't want to face up to. For instance, in *FOR BETTER OR WORSE*, Mike and Brian have organized a boys' club with "no girls aloud." "Headquarters" is inside a large box.

Brian: "It's gotta' be a million degrees inside this box, Mike. Let's get outa' here!"

Mike: "No way. As soon as we get out, Lizzie an' the girls will take it. I saw this refrigerator box first. It's *MINE*!!!"

Brian: "But we're gonna' croak in here! We could get heat frustration and die, man! This doesn't make sense!"

Mike: "This is war, Brian. It's not *SUPPOSED* to make sense!"

Two American Indians were talking things over in a fox-hole between air raids during World War II. "The way I figure it," one said, "is that when they smoked the peace pope in 1918, nobody inhaled!"

Someone asked Albert Einstein one day what kind of weapons would be used in the third World War. "Well," he answered, "I don't know...but I can tell you what they'll use in the fourth world war. They'll use rocks."

As someone has said, "Diplomacy is the art of saying, 'Nice doggie,' until you find a rock."

Perception

Many years ago, we had a rash of airplane hijackings in this country, particularly out of Miami airport. One such plane was hijacked on its way to New York. "Turn the plane around and head for Havana," ordered the hijacker gruffly. The pilot could tell that the man was desperate, so he did what the hijacker said. When the gunman tried to intimidate the passengers, however, they started roaring with laughter. No matter what the hijacker did, the passengers laughed. They laughed all the way to Havana. They laughed while the plane was on the ground and tense negotiations were going on between Cuban and American authorities. They laughed when the plane was allowed to resume its flight to New York. They turned the whole experience into a big party. Only one man was not laughing, besides the hijacker and the pilot. He didn't get the joke. In fact he was worried that the hijacker would react violently to the laughter of the other passengers. The whole experience was miserable for this one passenger. His name? Allen Funt, host of the popular *CANDID CAMERA*.

When the other passengers saw that Allen Funt was on board, they assumed this was all a prank. They were waiting for someone to say, "Surprise! You're on Candid Camera."

POLITICS

Humorist Robert Orben put it rightly sometime back, "Let him who is without sin contact the Democratic National committee."

Perhaps the greatest compliment ever paid President Grover Cleveland was when he was put in nomination before the Democratic Convention and the orator who presented his name said, "We love him for the enemies he has made."

There is a humorous story that comes out of John F. Kennedy's presidential campaign of 1960. After a stunning speech in San Antonio, Texas, to a large enthusiastic crowd assembled in front of the Alamo where a handful of Texans held off a large Mexican army, Kennedy wanted to make a quick exit. Turning to Maury Maverick, a local politician, he said, "Maury, let's get out of here. Where's the back door?" Maury replied, "Senator, if there had been a back door to the Alamo, there wouldn't have been any heroes."

Robert Orben says that the essence of America can be summed up in this exchange: A father told his son that all Americans belong to a privileged class. The son said, "I disagree." And the father said, "That's the privilege."

Some months after his defeat in the Presidential race of 1984, former Vice President Walter Mondale was giving a talk about terrorism at the American Bar Association convention in London. Suddenly there was an explosion. Security men jumped to their feet and the audience stiffened. It quickly became apparent that the noise had come from an exploding TV camera light. Unfortunately, this was immediately followed by fire sprinklers going into action, drenching the occupants of the room. Mondale looked around and then said, "Once you're out of office, you find there is very little dignity in this world."

The annual political conventions remind me of the story of the fellow in Vermont who said to his mother one day, "Mother, I don't believe you'd vote for God Himself if He ran on the Democratic ticket!" To which she replied: "Of course not; if He switched parties at this late date, he wouldn't be reliable!"

I once read a speech by a President of the United States (he's dead, so don't start guessing) in which he declared on page 1 that his religion was the Sermon on the Mount, and then on page 3, when dealing with foreign affairs, said: "Let's have no nonsense about turning the other cheek."
☞Dr. Donald Strobe

Belgium's Paul-Henri Spaak was presiding over the United Nations' first General Assembly. When it ended, he told his colleagues, "The agenda is exhausted. The Secretary-General is exhausted. I am exhausted. At last we have achieved unanimity!"

When the Soviet leader called President Reagan, a White House official rushed to the President and said, "Good news, Mr. President. General Secretary Gorvachev is calling to say he is in favor of free speech. The bad news is, he is calling collect."

Lyndon Johnson tried to get his fellow Democrats to put away regional differences. But then he added, "Of course, I do not want to go as far as the Georgia politician who shouted from the stump in the heat of debate, 'My fellow citizens, I know no North, I know no South, I know no East, I know no West.' A barefooted, freckle-faced boy shouted from the audience, 'Well, you better go back and study some geography!'"

Two old ladies were walking around a somewhat overcrowded English country churchyard and came upon a tombstone on which was the inscription: "Here lies John Smith, a politician and an honest man."

"Good heavens!" said one lady to the other. "Isn't it awful that they had to put two people in the same grave!"

An intriguing story appeared recently in "U.S.A. Today." It seems that a Miss Candy Postlethwaite received a sizeable check from the Veteran's Administration. That's not the strange part. The strange part is that the check was not made out to her, nor did she know the person to whom the check was made out to, nor had she ever been in the military.

She put it back outside for the postman to pick up on his next round. Five days later she got it back in a different envelope. She telephoned the VA office in her district and was directed to send the check there. She did--one week later she received the check back, in the same envelope. Next she mailed it to the Treasury Department office in Kansas City where the check was originally issued along with a certified letter advising that it did not belong to her and that she did not know the person to whom it had been issued. The check was returned to her in a different envelope.

Somewhat befuddled she took it next to the local postmaster. After explaining her situation to him, he advised her to give it to him for return to the Veteran's Administration. Relieved, she returned home. Two weeks later she received the check again! She was then instructed to mail it to Waco. It returned yet another time! After the seventh delivery she called the Dallas VA people and was told they didn't know what else they could do.

In desperation she called the secret service office and told one of the agents she intended to destroy the check. He informed her that to destroy the check would be against the law--it was government property! She told him she'd just cash it, to which he answered that she could not keep it either--it wasn't hers! The paper went on to say that she is awaiting further instructions. ∽ Don Emmitte

I personally wish that we had more presidents like Calvin Coolidge. Coolidge, frustrated with the idea of paying $25,000 for an *ENTIRE SQUADRON OF AIRCRAFT*, is said to have asked, "Why can't we just buy one aeroplane and let the aviators take turns flying it."

Calvin Coolidge was once asked, "Who lives in the White House?" He said, "Nobody. They keep coming and going."

President Lyndon Johnson insisted that Lawrence F. O'Brien take his oath of office as Postmaster General in a little post office in Hye, Texas, where he recalled mailing his first letter at the age of four. "It was about fifty-three years ago," said LBJ at the ceremony, "that I mailed my first letter from this post office. And Larry O'Brien told me a few moments ago that he is going out to find that letter and deliver it."

I don't recall the source of this, but back in the 1950 senatorial primary campaign in Florida, veteran Claude Pepper was opposed by George Smathers. Pepper was especially strong in the "Bible belt," or northern, section of Florida. To shake the hold Pepper had on these people, Smathers developed a special speech making use of the facts that Pepper, a Harvard Law School graduate, has a niece who was a staff member of a Senate Subcommittee, and a sister who acted in New York.

For the county courthouse rallies, Smathers would say, "Are you aware, my friends, that in his youth Claude Pepper was found matriculating in Harvard, that before marriage he habitually indulged in celibacy. Not only that, he was practicing nepotism in Washington with his own niece; and he has a sister who is a thespian in wicked Greenwich Village. Worst of all, my friends, Claude Pepper is known all over Washington for his latent tendency toward overt extraversion."

POSITIVE THINKING

A group of new recruits was going through basic training in World War II. Unfortunately, there were not enough rifles to go around.

The sergeant gave a very gullible young man from the Tennesse mountains a broomstick instead and told him, "When you need to shoot, just point this and say, 'Bangity, bangity, bang!'"

There was not even a bayonet for the young soldier so the sergeant, tying a stick to the end of the broom, said, "If you get into hand-to-hand combat just poke the enemy with this and say 'stabbity, stabbity, stab!'"

The young mountain lad was nervous, but he figured the sergeant knew what he was doing. Finally, the company was in combat. Sure enough, the young soldier with the broomstick saw a few German soldiers running toward his position. He pointed the broomstick at them and said, "Bangity, bangity, bang!" He was amazed when they all fell down. Suddenly another soldier jumped out from behind a nearby tree. Immediately the mountian boy poked him with the stick and said, "Stabbity, stabbity, stab!" The German fell at his feet. Just then another enemy approached, so he pointed his broomstick and shouted confidently, "Bangity, bangity, bang!" This time, however, the German just kept on coming. So the young fellow poked him with the stick and said, "Stabbity, stab-bity, stab!" But he just kept on coming.

Finally the German knocked the young man down and walked over him. As the young man was lying on his back being trampled, he heard the German saying, "Tankity, tankity, tank!"

Yes, positive thinking only goes so far.

Ruth Baldwin in *CATHOLIC DIGEST* tells about an experience she had with her four-year-old daughter. The mother, a devout Roman Catholic, had been praying the Rosary each evening after she finished the supper dishes. After watching a few times, her four-year-old daughter asked if she could pray with her. So the mother explained to her that she would say the first part of the prayer and the little girl could finish it. Since the child did not know the prayers, her mother recited them with her a few times until the little girl said, "I can do it now."

Her mother began, and when she had prayed the first half of the *GLORIA PATRI*, (Glory be to the Father, and to the Son and to the Holy Ghost) she waited for the little girl to finish with, "As it was in the beginning, is now, and ever shall be." Instead, the little girl devoutly answered, "It's better now than it was before!"

When I addressed an audience of doctors in San Diego, one of them assured me he was the hero of the story, widely circulated, about an operation on a bad-tempered lady of about eighty. She came through with flying colors despite all her dire prognostications, but set up a new clamor when the doctor told her that in accordance with the rules of the hospital, she'd have to walk ten minutes the very first day after her surgery and would have to get out entirely in a week, since beds there were at a premium.

Well, she had her ten-minute walk the first day, tottering but under her own steam, lengthened it to twenty minutes the second day, and by the time she went home, was stomping all over the hospital--including rooms where she had no right to be.

Later her family tried to pay the doctor a premium for his "wonderful job."

"Nonsense," he laughed. "It was a routine operation."

"It's not the operation we're marveling over," said a grandson. "It's her walking. The old girl hadn't taken a step in six years!" ∞ Bennett Cerf

Somewhere I read a story about an American serviceman who was stationed deep in the Sahara Desert. Finding himself with a few hours to kill, he put on his swimming trunks and began trudging merrily through the desert sand. One of his buddies asked in astonishment, "Where do you think you are going?" The carefree soldier replied, "Well, I've got a few hours of leave and I thought I would take a dip in the surf." His buddy laughed at him and said, "Are you crazy? We are 500 miles from the ocean." His undaunted friend replied, "I know--but isn't this the biggest, most beautiful beach you have ever seen?"

Someone asked a football coach, "How do you keep your spirits up when your team is losing?" He shrugged and replied, "I'm the kind of guy who, if I fell in a mud puddle, would get up and feel in my pockets for fish."

Charlie Pell, Clemson football coach, said it best. Above all, he demanded attitude coupled with action from his players. "I want them to think as positively as the eighty-five-year-old man who married a twenty-five-year-old woman and ordered a five-bedroom house near an elementary school."

In a *FRANK AND ERNEST* cartoon, you see Frank rousing slowly from his sleep, then looking out at the sun coming up. He says dryly, "Well, the sun is rising in the east...so far, so good."

There is a delightful story about a young lady on a cruise ship who kept glancing at an attractive young man. He could not help but notice her attention and was flattered. Finally he mustered up the courage to approach her. "Pardon me," he said with a gentle smile. "It may be my imagination, but I could not help but noticing that you keep looking in my direction. Is there something wrong?" She blushed and said demurely, "Oh, no. It's just that I can't help but notice how much you resemble my first husband." The young man looked puzzled and asked, "How many times have you been married?" She gave a mysterious smile and answered, "Oh, I haven't been yet."

It is so easy for us to take it all for granted, like the woman who said, "Well, that's a rather lovely sunset for such a little town!"

POTENTIAL

There is a true story about a very diplomatic young man who arrived unannounced at a certain young lady's house. She came to the door with her hair "teased" in about six million directions. Her hair looked like she might have accidentally inserted her finger in a light socket. It was a very awkward moment. There was nothing she could do but try to make light of the situation, so she asked good-naturedly, "How do you like my hair?" He stood there for a moment and then replied, "It looks as if it's about to become something wonderful."

PRAYER

There was a cartoon sometime back in which a little fellow said with disgust, "Uncle Jim still doesn't have a job, Sis still doesn't have a date for that prom, Grandma is still feeling poorly. I'm tired of praying for this family and not getting results."

When Sally in the *PEANUTS* strip was called on in Sunday School to lead her class in prayer, she adapted the only prayer she knew: "Now I lay us down to sleep...."

Edith Bunker, on the television show "All in the Family," described the confessional boxes in the Roman Catholic Church as "telephone booths to God."

There is a story about a very dignified pastor who was visiting a lady in a nursing home who was confined to a wheel chair. As he stood to leave, the lady asked him to have a word of prayer. He gently took her hand and prayed that God would be with her to bring her comfort, strength and healing. When he finished praying her face began to glow. She said softly, "Pastor, would you help me to my feet?" Not knowing what else to do, he helped her up. At first, she took a few uncertain steps. Then she began to jump up and down, then to dance and shout and cry with happiness until the whole nursing home was aroused. After she was quieted, the solemn pastor hurried out to his car, closed the door, grabbed hold of the steering wheel and prayed a little prayer, "Lord, don't you ever do that to me again!"

The *CHRISTIAN CENTURY* recently printed an amusing account of a high school football team in the San Fernando Valley of California that is defying the ban on prayer in public schools.

Bob Francola, coach of the Kennedy High School Cougars, said that his team has modified the practice to remove any religious references from its prayers. "I am still allowed to have a quiet moment with our team," he said, "so instead I just ask the Big Cougar in the sky to help us out."

A man came home drunk after a night of carousing in a number of neighborhood bars. His wife helped him up to the bedroom, helped him to undress and tucked him into bed. Then she kneeled at his bedside and whispered, "John, do you want me to pray for you?" He nodded a yes and she began to pray, "Dear Lord, I pray for my husband who lies here before you drunk..." Before she could finish, he interrupts. Don't tell Him I'm drunk," he pleads, "Just tell Him I'm sick."

It is said that one of President's Reagan's favorite stories is the one about the minister's son who was taken out camping one day. His companion warned him not to stray too far from the campfire because the woods were full of wild beasts of all kinds. The young boy had every intention, of following that advice but inevitably was drawn by curiosity and wandered farther and farther from the fire. Suddenly he found himself face to face with a very large and powerful looking bear. He saw no means of escape, and seeing the bear advance rather menacingly towards him, the miniter's son did what he had been taught to do. He knelt down to pray for deliverance. He closed his eyes tightly, but opened them a few moments later and was delighted to see that the bear was also kneeling in prayer right in front of him. He said, "Oh, bear, isn't this wonderful! Here we are with such different view points and such different lives and such different perceptions of life and we're both praying to the same Lord!" The bear said evenly, "Son, I don' t know about you, but I'm saying grace."

We are like the five-year-old, who told his dad he'd like to have a baby brother. His dad thought for a moment and then replied, "I'll tell you what. If every night for two months you pray for a baby brother, I guarantee that God will give you one!" Dad knew something that little Bobby didn't.

That night this young boy went to his bedroom early to start praying for a baby brother. He prayed every night for a whole month, but then he began to get a little weary. He quit praying for a baby brother. After another month, however, his mother went to the hospital. When she came back home, his parents called him into the bedroom. When he came in he saw a little bundle lying right next to his mother. His dad pulled back the blanket and there were, not just one baby brother, but two baby brothers--twins! Bobby's dad looked down at him and said, "Now, aren't you glad you prayed?"

Young Bobby hesitated a little and then looked up at his dad and answered, "Yes, but aren't you glad I quit when I did?"

A mother was listening to her little boy say his prayers. "Thank you, Father, for Mommy, Daddy...and please make St. Louis the Capital of Missouri."

His surprised mother asked, "Why did you pray for St. Louis to be the capital of Missouri?"

"Because that's the answer I put on my test."

Actor Dick Van Dyke tells the story of a little girl who is asked by her mother if she had said her night-time prayers. "Yes, mother," she replies. "But when I got down on my knees, I began thinking that God hears the same old stuff every night. So I told him the story of *THE THREE BEARS* instead."

There is a story about a little boy who was praying: "Now I lay me down to sleep. I pray the Lord my soul to keep." Then there was a long pause. He couldn't remember what came next. His mother sought to prompt him from the doorway. "If," she said quietly. The little boy prayed, "If...if..." Then he brightened up and said triumphantly, "If he hollers let him go, Eeny, meeny, miny, mo!"

One little fellow prayed, "Our Father who art in heaven, who hollered my name?"

PREPARATION

A young man asked his sweetheart to marry him, and she happily accepted on the condition that he save $1,000. So he got a job in another city and promised to be back shortly. Time dragged on and the girl fretted because she had not heard from him in almost a year. Finally he came back. Overjoyed that they could now proceed with their plans, she asked him, "Have you saved the thousand dollars?"

"No," he replied, dejected. "I've only saved thirty-five dollars so far."

"Well," she answered, happy nonetheless, "that's near enough. Let's get married."

The new music teacher at the Junior High school had just organized a band. The principal decided that the band should give its first concert, but the music teacher was not certain that the band was ready. Just before the concert, the music teacher whispered to her nervous musicians, "If you're not sure of your part, just pretend to play."

When the big moment arrived, she brought her baton down with a sweeping flourish and lo, nothing happened. The band gave forth with a resounding silence.

Two soldiers penetrated deeply into a hostile country on a highly dangerous sabotage mission. They were captured by an army patrol and immediately brought before a firing squad. They were bound, blindfolded, and surrounded by an entire company of soldiers with automatic rifles poised. The command was given: "Ready, aim..." At this point one of the doomed soldiers turned to his partner and whispered, "I've got a plan."

PRIDE

People are funny. They spend money they don't have to buy things they don't need to impress people they don't like.

I like a very proper blue-blooded English officer's summary of World War II: "My dear, the noise! And the people!"

Wasn't it Mark Twan who said he spent a large sum of money to trace his family tree and then spent twice as much trying to keep his ancestry a secret?

PURPOSE

We are often like the fellow I saw in a cartoon many years ago. It showed an historical scene, the runner from the Battle of Marathon bringing news of the victory to Athens. A group of Athenian city fathers was waiting in strained anxiety. The runner arrived, carrying a torch, and gasped out, "I've forgotten the message."

One cold February day a snail started climbing an apple tree. As he inched slowly upward, a worm stuck its head from a crevice in the tree to offer some advice. "You're wasting your energy. There isn't a single apple up there."

The snail kept up his slow climb. "There will be when I get there," he said.

In the *PEANUTS* cartoon series Lucy is in business as a psychiatrist. "Advice--5 cents," says her sign. Charlie Brown is her client. "Lucy, I need help," he says woefully. "What can I do for a purpose in life?" Lucy responds, "Oh, don't worry, Charlie. It's like being on a big ocean liner making its way through the sea. Some folks put their deck chairs to face the bow of the ship, and others place their chairs to face the side of the ship or the back of the ship. Which way do you face, Charlie?" Charlie Brown concludes sadly, "I can't even unfold the deck chair."

Tim Timmons tells about an interesting piece of graffiti that he once saw. Someone had drawn a radio with a message coming out of the speaker. The message said, "This life is a test. It is only a test. Had this been an actual life you would have received instructions as to what to do and where to go."

Someone has said life is like a taxi ride. The meter keeps ticking whether you are getting anywhere or not.

Three men went on a fishing trip. Their boat was wrecked in a storm, but they managed to swim to a deserted island. After a week, one of the three, a cattle baron, became despondent; he missed his ranch. A second longed for his native Manhattan, where he was a cab driver. The third man, a happy-go-lucky type, was enjoying himself, finding the experience rather peaceful. One day, as they were walking along the beach, the carefree fellow happened to see an ancient lamp which he promptly picked up. He rubbed it and a genie sprang out. "For freeing me from my prison," said the genie, "each of you shall receive one wish." "I'd like to be back on my ranch," said the cattle baron, quick to grab the opportunity. Poof! He was gone! "I'd like to be driving my hack again," said the cabby. Poof! He was gone! "And what is your wish?" asked the genie of the third man, who by then was looking a little forlorn. "Well," he said, "I'm kinda lonely now without the other guys. I wish they were back." Poof! Poof! ∞ Donald W. Morgan, *How to Get It Together When Your World is Coming Apart,* (Old Tappan, N.J.: Fleming H. Revell, 1988).

A boy received a nice guitar for Christmas. He put his hands on the fret and held it in one fixed position while he strummed on the instrument hour upon hour. His father became vexed with him and said, "Son, you are supposed to move your left hand up and down the neck of the guitar and produce new sounds. Chet Atkins and Les Paul, the great guitarists, do that." The little boy replied, "Well, Dad, they run their left hand up and down because they are still looking for it--I found it."

RELIGION

Robert Short, author of *THE GOSPEL ACCORDING TO PEANUTS* AND *PARABLES OF PEANUTS,* tells how as a high school student in Midland, Texas, he became an agnostic, though he was raised in a Methodist home. He became president of a science club that caused such a controversy that his high school principal complained to his parents. He tells how he sat across from his mother who, with tears running down her face said, "I thought we raised you right. I never thought it would come to this--our son an agnostic."

Later Robert Short found a new relationship to Jesus Christ in college and felt a call to the ministry. At home he told his mother of his decision. Sitting at that same kitchen table, with tears running down her cheeks, she said, "I never thought it would come to this--my son, a religious fanatic."

Life is a mystery. It's like the Eskimo who went on a visit for the first time to New York City. When he returned to his home, he brought with him a large box. His curious family opened the box to discover a rather strange looking metal frame. "What is it?" they asked. "It's a radiator. It's a great invention," he said. "They use it in New York. You prop it upright in the bedroom. When you have a very cold night, you rap on it and you get heat."

Or it's like some mice that had made a nest in a certain piano. When they heard music, they decided to investigate. One mouse came back and reported that the music came from various lengths of strings. Another claimed the music came from the hammers. They heard the music but they never saw the "invisible" pianist. And of course mice are not bright enough to conclude that the pianist exists. Some people are not either!

A recent widower gave these instructions to the stonemason who was preparing the tombstone for his late wife: "I want 'Rest in Peace' on both sides. Then, if there's enough room: 'We shall meet in heaven.'" After the memorial stone had been erected, he read the following:

> Rest in peace on both sides
> And if there is enough room,
> We shall meet in heaven.

A passenger reported recently being on a plane that appeared to be ready for takeoff when there was a loud and persistent banging on the aircraft door. Finally the crew checked, and found that the banging was being caused by the captain of the plane, who had somehow been locked out. Maybe that's what's happened to our world today. We've locked out the captain!

There was a believer who was not everything he ought to be and he knew it! In fact, when he finally passed from this life to the next one he was deeply concerned that St. Peter wouldn't let him through the Pearly Gates. When he got to his destination, however, he was welcomed with open arms.

"Are you certain that you didn't make a mistake?" he asked St. Peter. "You see, there are certain parts of my life of which I'm sort of ashamed."

St. Peter answered, "No, we didn't make a mistake. You see, we don't keep any records."

The man was greatly relieved and overjoyed. Then he saw a group of men over in a corner beating their heads against a celestial wall and clinching their fists and stomping their feet in disgust. "What is the matter with them?" the man asked St. Peter.

"Oh", said St. Peter with a smile. "They also thought we kept records."

Father John Powell in his book, *UNCONDITIONAL LOVE,* tells about when he was serving as a chaplain in Germany. A dear little sister, 87 years young, was assigned to care for his room. He says that every time he left the room, even for a moment, the good sister cleaned it. She would wax the floors, polish the furniture and so forth. On one occasion when he left the room for a short walk, he came back to find her on her knees putting a final sheen on her waxing job. He laughingly teased her, "Sister, you work too much." The dear, devoted little sister straightened up (though still kneeling) and looked at him with a seriousness that bordered on severity. She said firmly, "Heaven isn't cheap, you know."

I heard an amusing story about a group of Methodists who were holding a camp meeting. Some top flight preachers from across the country were coming in to share in this event. One of the main speakers was forced, at the very last minute, to cancel out. He was supposed to preach right after lunch that day and they had no speaker.

So the Bishop went to a young pastor with a lot of promise and said, "I want you to fill in and preach in that service after lunch."

The young pastor said, "Well, Bishop! How can I do that? I didn't bring any sermons with me. I came strictly to listen and to worship. How could I possibly get up there and deliver a sermon to this large congregation?"

The Bishop said, "Son, just trust the Lord. Trust the Lord."

The pastor was dumbfounded. In his despair he saw the Bishop's Bible on a shelf nearby. He went over and started thumbing through it trying to find a text from which he could somehow draw a message.

While he was thumbing through the Bishop's Bible he came across a set of notes. He realized that this was the address that the Bishop was to give that night. The time grew closer and the young man was getting more and more desperate. So when the time came for the service, the young man took the Bishop's notes and preached the Bishop's sermon.

The response was overwhelming. Everybody came up and congratulated him and told him what a wonderful sermon it was. It was an exciting moment until the Bishop came up, and he was furious.

He said, "Young man! What have you done? You have preached the sermon I was going to preach tonight. What am I going to do now?"

The young pastor looked up with a twinkle in his eye and said, "Trust the Lord, Bishop. Just trust the Lord."

The "Wesleyan Revival" of the 18th century came on the wings of song. When John and Charles Wesley were criticized for setting some of their hymns to popular drinking song tunes of the day, they replied that they did not see why the Devil should have all of the good tunes!

A certain man loved to go to revivals. He loved to get up and testify. He made his witness over and over again, publicly admitting his past sinful life. He had done it all--lied, cheated, stolen, pushed dope, spent time in jail, broken all the Ten Commandments and then some! It was his custom at the end of his long recital of wrongdoing to smile and say, "I thank God through all those wicked years I never lost my religion."

A rich asbestos manufacturer built a fine house just across the street from the minister. The manufacturer and his family then proceeded to enjoy themselves in what the minister thought to be a very worldly fashion, and not once did he see them in church. But the minister was never known to speak ill of anyone. He only said to his wife, "Dear me, they must have a great deal of faith in their asbestos."

A plaque in a pastor's office: "If you have the joy of Jesus please notify your face."

High up in the mountains she saw a woman sitting on a front porch. She parked her car and walked over to speak to the woman.
"Madam, are there any Evangelicals in this section?" she asked the one who was rocking.
"I don't know for sure," came the reply, "but if there have been any you'll find their hides nailed to the barn door. My husband is a crack shot."

C. S. Lewis was asked why so many Christians seem less than perfect. He replied, "You should have seen them *BEFORE* they became Christians."

It is said the difference between Baptists and Methodists is that the Methodists have salvation but are afraid they might lose it. The Baptists know you can't lose it, but are afraid they may not have it.

J. Wallace Hamilton once told a story about a Russian girl who was brought up as an atheist. She had taken a government examination, and like all students, was worried about some of the answers she had given. One particular question on the exam had bothered her. The question was this: "What is the inscription of the Samarian Wall?" She had written the answer: "Religion is the opiate of the people"--that famous anti-religion declaration of Karl Marx. But the girl wasn't sure of her answer, so she walked seven miles to the Samarian Wall to check it out and sure enough, there it was: "Religion is the opiate of the people." Greatly relieved, she forgot for a moment her upbringing, and said, "Thank God! I had it right."

As a theology professor of mine used to say: "If there isn't a devil, there's sure somebody getting his work done for him!"

A farmer once had a fine ewe which gave birth to two lambs. When one lamb died the farmer remarked, "Well, it's all for the best. I'd rather have one fat lamb than two skinny ones." Still later, the other lamb died, and he reflected, "Well, it's all for the best. Now the ewe won't be bothered with them." When a week later the ewe died, the farmer was still philosophical. "Well, it's all for the best," said he, "but I'll be darned if I can figure it out."

A rabbi and a soapmaker went for a walk together. The soapmaker said, "What good is religion? Look at all the trouble and misery of the world! Still there, even after years--thousands of years--of teaching about goodness and truth and peace. Still there, after all the prayers and sermons and teachings. If religion is good and true, why should this be?"

The rabbi said nothing. They continued walking until he noticed a child playing in the gutter.

Then the rabbi said, "Look at that child. You say that soap makes people clean, but see the dirt on that youngster. Of what good is soap? With all the soap in the world, over all these years, the child is still filthy. I wonder how effective soap is, after all!"

The soapmaker protested. "But, Rabbi, soap cannot do any good unless it is used!"

"Exactly," replied the Rabbi. "Exactly!" ᴏ⊛ Norm Lawson

When Oliver Cromwell first coined his money, an old Cavalier, looking at one of the new pieces, read this inscription on one side, "God is with us." On the other, "The Commonwealth of England."

"I see," said he, "that God and the Commonwealth are on different sides."

Dr. T.R. Glover liked to quote a little boy who said that the Bible began with Genesis and ended in Revolutions!

Warren Wiersbe tells the story of the pious church member who upon visiting the sixth grade Sunday school class asked, "Why do you think people call me a Christian?" There was an embarrassing silence, then a small voice from the back of the class said, "Because they don't know you."

In the South they tell about a certain man's son who was sent to the penitentiary. The boy wrote his father, "In here, Daddy, it's just like it is out there. Us Baptists is in the lead."

Dr. Gus McLean, a Presbyterian church pastor, chastised his young son for fighting a public school classmate who was Jewish. He said, "Son, you ought to be ashamed of yourself. Don't you know that Jesus was a Jew?"

"Father, I'm sorry," his son replied. "I know God is a Presbyterian, but I had no idea that Jesus was a Jew."

RESPONSIBILITY

A young Navy pilot was engaged in maneuvers. The admiral had required absolute radio silence. However, the young pilot mistakenly turned on his radio and was heard to mutter, "Boy, am I fouled up!" The admiral grabbed the mike, ordered all channels to be opened, and said, "Will the pilot who broke the radio silence identify himself immediately!" A long silence ensued before a small voice was heard over the airways: "I am fouled up, but not that fouled up!"

We can sympathize with the poor man who went to a psychologist and said, "Doc, I'm ready to end it all. I have nothing to live for anymore." The doctor said, "What do you mean you have nothing to live for. Your house isn't paid for. Your television isn't paid for. Your furniture isn't paid for. You haven't paid me for this visit. What do you mean that you haven't got anything to live for?"

The wreck of a 17th Century Spanish Galleon was discovered off the coast of Florida. To play it safe Exxon has already denied any responsibility. ➣ Gary Apple, *Current Comedy*

Are you like James R. Bailey, the Superintendent of the Fort Worth, Texas, public schools? Meeting one day with a city-wide Parent-Teachers' Association, Bailey sought to communicate openness and accessibility. He told the audience he would be pleased to speak with them any hour of the day or night. "In fact," he said, "here's the telephone number..." and proceeded to recite it. There was a sudden outcry from Assistant Superintendent Joe Ross. "Hey!" Ross shouted, "That's my number you're giving out!"

Some enterprising dorm sisters had a system for dealing with the problem of what to do when the wrong fellow called asking for a date. They put together a list of ten excuses and taped it next to the phone. That way they could decline an invitation without fumbling around for an excuse. It worked like a charm. Except for the time one flustered girl was overheard saying, "I'd love to go out with you, Tom, but I can't because, uh, because Number Seven."

Charlie Brown's dog Snoopy is playing tennis. In picture one, Snoopy is shown with a brand new tennis racket. However, things are not going well. He is angry. In fact we see him throw his racket to the court, kick it and stomp on it. Finally, in great anguish he smashes it over the tennis net pole. In the final frame of the cartoon he is seen addressing a letter: "Gentlemen, under separate cover I am returning a defective tennis racket."

A sailor was leaning on the deck rail when his buddy stuck his head up through a nearby hatch. "The ship is sinking!" his buddy cried.
The sailor shrugged. "So what? It's not my ship."

RISK

The little fellow in the comic strip ZIGGY, a philosopher of a sort, once said, "Security is knowing what tomorrow will bring. Boredom is knowing what the day after tomorrow will bring."

Sex

Gloria: Then you know what I mean?

Edith: Oh, yea...when you was a baby, I had the same problem, but I couldn't talk to my mother. In those day, we didn't even have books like *EVERYTHING YOU ALWAYS WANTED TO KNOW ABOUT (UH) BUT WAS AFRAID TO ASK."*

Gloria: Did you read that book?

Edith: Oh, no.

Gloria: So you still don't know everything?

Edith: No, and I'm still afraid to ask. ☞ Spencer Marsh, *Edith the Good* (New York: Harper & Row Publishers, 1977).

Entering a hospital room, the doctor was surprised to find the nurse holding his patient by both wrists. "That's not the way to check his pulse," chided the doctor.

"I'm not checking his pulse," the nurse replied. "I'm checking his impulse."

Sin

Mrs. Billie Cannon--a Knoxville, Tennessee, homemaker, was preparing to paint her back porch. In order to protect the floor, she very carefully placed around the edges a strip of Scotch tape--the kind with adhesive on both sides. It was her plan to place a drop cloth over the floor and secure it with the tape. Having succeeded in placing the tape around the entire surface, she went back inside the house to get a drop cloth. Returning to the porch sometime later, she found that all of her carefully placed tape was gone. She was completely mystified. Where could it be? Who would possibly have taken the time to pull up that tape and why? As she was surveying the situation and mulling over her puzzling predicament, she noticed something moving in her back yard. Looking closer she discovered that it was a snake. It was a rather large creature of its species, but it was no threat to her. It was hopelessly immobilized by being totally enmeshed in a large ball of Scotch tape. Evidently, while Mrs. Cannon was in the house the snake had crawled up on the back porch and had eased itself onto that tape with the adhesive on both sides. Sensing that the tape was sticking to its skin, the snake obviously put up a terrible struggle. In doing so it pulled every bit of tape from the floor. The harder it fought, however, the more hopelessly it became entangled in its cellophane prison until now it was totally captive. ∽ A true story related by her pastor, the Rev. Jerry Anderson, Cokesbury United Methodist Church, Knoxville, Tenn.

There is a cartoon which has appeared in several religious periodicals. It shows a crucifixion scene, and depicts Jesus as saying: "If I'm O.K. and you're O.K., what am I doing hanging on this cross?"

A burly lineman for a professional football team often stayed out late, despite the club's curfew. He would pile things under his blankets, making it appear he was in bed.
At one hotel, however, he couldn't find enough things to stuff the bed with. So he stuck a floor lamp under the covers and departed. When a suspicious coach peeked in at 1 a.m. and snapped on the light switch, the bed lit up. ∽ Raymond Schuessler in *Modern Maturity*

SOLUTION

In his book *FATHER CARE* (Waco: Word Books, 1983), Charles Paul Conn tells about his two-year-old daughter Vanessa who was given a helium-filled balloon at Sunday

School. It was bright blue and seemed almost alive as it danced and floated on the end of her string as she ran through the halls of the church pulling it along behind her. But the inevitable happened. The balloon bumped into the sharp edge of a metal railing and popped. With a single, loud "bang" it burst and fell to her feet. She looked down and saw what had been her beautiful balloon, now a forlorn wad of wet blue rubber. It took her only a moment to regain her buoyant mood, however, as she picked up the remains of that balloon, marched cheerfully to where her father was standing and thrust it up to him. "Here, Daddy," she said brightly. "Fix it."

"Doctor, I'm always worried about my baby," said the young mother to the psychistrist. "I'm afraid to leave him alone for even a minute. For example, I'm even afraid to leave him in the bedroom for fear I won't hear him if he falls out of his crib."

"Well, you can remedy that easily," said the doctor. "Just take the carpet off the floor."

There is a silly story about a man who went to his doctor complaining about terrible neck pains, throbbing headaches, shortness of breath, visual blurring, and recurring dizzy spells. The doctor examined him and said, "I'm afraid I have some bad news for you. You have only six months to live."

The doomed man decided he would spend his remaining time on earth enjoying himself. He quit his job, bought a sports car, and a closet full of new suits and shoes.

Then he went to get himself a dozen tailored shirts. He went to the finest shirt shop he could find. The tailor measured him and wrote down "size 16 neck."

"Wait a moment," the man injected. "I always wear a size 14 neck, and that is what I want."

"I'd be glad to do it for you, sir," the tailor replied. "However, if you wear a size 14 neck I can guarantee you that you're going to have terrible neck pains, throbbing headaches, shortness of breath, visual blurring, and recurring dizzy spells."

An insurance agent filed this claim on behalf of one of his clients: "The Insured operates a dude ranch and we insure all of his ranch buildings and his pickup truck. He had been having trouble with coyotes and had rigged up an ingenious sapling cage trap to catch the animals, after which he would shoot them. This time he decided to try something different, and instead of shooting the coyote, he tied a stick of dynamite to its neck and lit the fuse, opening the cage door at the same time. The coyote unobligingly ran under the Insured's pickup truck. The claim is for the truck which is a total loss." ↬ Brian Herbert, *Incredible Insurance Claims* (Los Angeles: Price, Stern, Sloan Publishers, 1982).

Will Rogers was attributed with a unique way to solve the German U-boat menace in World War I. He suggested that the temperature of the ocean be raised until it was unbearably hot. This would force the submarines to surface, where they could easily be destroyed.

"But how can you possibly heat up the ocean water to that degree?" he was asked.

"I've given you the concept," Will replied. "It's up to you to work out the details."

SPEAKING

Once asked his secret for success, a well-known speaker said, "First, have an attention- grabbing opening for your speech---something that will attract everyone. Always have a thorough, dramatic summary and a conclusion that leaves your audience interested. Then, you put them as close together as possible."

The mind is a wonderful thing. It starts working the minute you are born and only stops when you get up to make a speech.

Kevin Murphy, in his recent book, *EFFECTIVE LISTENING,* tells of a speaker that he knew, from the moment he took his place on the dais, was someone he wanted to speak to face-to- face. He clearly had learned speaking skills. Murphy writes:

"His poise was remarkable; his message--on sharpening communication skills--was electrifying.

"But as soon as I introduced myself to this self-professed 'listening colleague,' he launched into a monologue on his background, qualifications, and successes. I felt my eyes glaze over and my attention start to wander. Moments later, I 'came to,' embarrassed for my end of the communication failure.

"'I'm sorry,' I offered. 'I didn't catch that last sentence.'

"'Oh, uh, right,' he stammered. 'What was I saying?'"
∞ David W. Richardson

A boring speaker is one who doesn't know when to quip.
∞ Eric Shively

Auditorium. The word has two Latin parts: "audio," meaning "hear" and "taurus," meaning "bull."

A public speaker was rushed to the hospital in an emergency, and a nurse, fresh from school was assigned to him. Instead of a thermometer, she put a barometer in his mouth. When she took a reading it said, "Dry and windy."

A gifted speaker was asked what was his most difficult speaking assignment. He said that it was an address he gave to the National Conference of Undertakers entitled "How to Look Sad at a Ten-Thousand Dollar Funeral."

Good opener at a banquet: "Before I begin, I'd like to tell you the name of that main course you just had for lunch--in case they ask you when you get to the hospital."

A story has been told of the late Judge Vincent, one of several speakers on a banquet program years ago in Chicago. Although he had expected to be called upon shortly after eleven, it was almost two o'clock in the morning when the poor man's turn came. The toastmaster, the late Mayor Moses Handy, is reported to have introduced his Honor as follows:

"And now we come to the final speaker on this remarkable program. I would be only too happy to give him the laudatory introduction he so richly deserves, but because of the lateness of the hour, I do not wish to deprive the speaker of one moment of his allotted time, nor the ladies and gentlemen in the audience of a moment of their enjoyment. I shall, therefore, content myself with saying that Judge Vincent will now give his address."

The Judge arose and said, "My address is 2137 Calumet Avenue. Thank you and good night." ∞ Steve Allen, *How to Make a Speech*, (New York: McGraw-Hill. 1985).

Good Closing: The story is told about a young country fellow who was walking with his girl on a moonlit night. He was overcome with the romance of the moment and he blurted out, "Honey, I love you so much. Will you marry me?" She did not hesitate. "Of course, I will marry you," she said joyfully. They walked along for a little while longer in silence and she said, "Dearest, why don't you say something?" He looked at the ground and said, "I think I've said too much as it is."

BREVITY: THE OXFORD DICTIONARY OF QUOTATIONS cites the anonymous "On the Antiquity of Microbes" as the shortest poem ever written. It consists of three words: Adam Had'em.

An outstanding speaker was scheduled to address a university audience.About two hours before she was to speak, however, a couple of student pranksters loaded a truck with all of the folding chairs in the auditorium and drove off.

No one was aware of this until the audience began to gather for the lecture. It was too late to do anything about it, and the audience was forced to stand throughout her talk.

That evening she wrote a letter to her mother: "It was a tremendous success. I was given a standing ovation when I was introduced and a standing ovation when I finished. Not only that, but hours before I got there every seat in the house was taken."

TAXES

Someone has said, "You may not agree with every department in the government, but you really have to hand it to the IRS."

Benjamin Franklin said that "in this world nothing is certain but death and taxes." A cynic has said, "Death and taxes may always be with us, but at least death doesn't get any worse."

Arthur Godfrey once said, "I feel honored to pay taxes in America. The thing is, I could probably feel just as honored for about half the price."

According to ancient tradition, the Gospel of Matthew was written by a tax-collector, and if this is true, the clarity and the simplicity of this Gospel comes as a surprise to anyone who reads it. Imagine, a Gospel written by a tax-collector! What do you suppose a gospel written by the IRS might sound like today?

"Once there was an adult male named Joseph, a self-employed carpenter with two dependents, Mary, who was an unemployed housekeeper, and a minor son named Jesus. Jesus was born six days before December ended, and this provided Joseph with a full deduction for the entire year. Jesus was born in Bethlehem while Joseph and Mary were on a business-related trip, which could not be deducted. The family received considerable assets of gold, frankincense, and myrrh while in Bethlehem, and a ruling has not yet been made on whether this increase in net worth should be reported as income on line 12, page 2." ∾ Dr. Eugene W. Brice, *Books That Bring Life*, Vol. 2. (Lubbock, TX.: Net Press, 1987).

Someone has noted that besides being income tax day, April 15 is also the day the Titanic sunk and the day that Lincoln was shot.

ℐELEVISION

Television is a tremendous cultural homogenizer. The secular values formerly associated primarily with our great cities are brought into nearly every home in America every day. A teacher at recess asked a little boy if he knew about "ring-around-the-rosy." He replied, "No, but I know about ring around the collar."

Do people take what they view on television too seriously? The answer is "yes." For example, several years ago on "The Edge of Night," two of the leading characters got married. The details of the wedding were so real and so complete that 576 gifts were received as wedding presents from the viewing audience. Some were minor and insignificant, but a number of them involved sustantial expense.

TEMPTATION

Continental Cablevision of Madison Heights, Michigan, had a little trouble with some of its electronic switching equipment, resulting in X-rated programming being fed into the homes of many subscribers who hadn't ordered it. The alarm was sounded by a scandalized customer who called a local radio station to say, "It was really awful--we saw it for four hours."

An overweight businessman decided to shed some excess pounds. He took his new diet seriously, even changing his driving route to avoid his favorite bakery. One morning, however, he arrived at work carrying a gigantic coffeecake. Everyone in the office scolded him, but his smile remained cherubic.

"This is very special coffeecake," he explained. "I accidently drove by the bakery this morning and there in the window were a host of goodies. I felt this was no accident, so I prayed, "Lord, if you want me to have one of these delicious coffeecakes, let me have a parking place directly in front of the bakery. And sure enough," he continued, "the eighth time around the block, there it was!"

A cartoon showed a man dressed like a prophet carrying a sign on which was written *RESIST TEMPTATION*. A rather seedy looking character saw the sign and responded, "I'm not interested in resisting it. I'm interested in finding it."

I can appreciate the story of a little boy named Bobby who badly wanted a new bicycle. His plan was to save his nickels, dimes, and quarters until he finally had enough to buy a new 10-speed. Each night he took his concern to the Lord. Kneeling beside his bed, he prayed, "Lord, please help me save for my new bicycle and please Lord, don't let the ice cream man come down our street tomorrow."

Anthony Evans in *PREACHING TODAY* tells a great story about a forester named Sam. Old Sam would be out chopping down the tree. You could hear him say one phrase: "Oh, Adam. Oh, Adam." Every time he hit that tree, he'd say, "Oh, Adam."

One day the foreman came by and asked him, "How come every time you hit the tree, you say, 'Oh, Adam?'" Sam said, "Because Adam, my forefather, sinned against God. God cursed him and said that he would have to work from that time on. So every time I hit this ax against the tree, it reminds me that if Adam hadn't sinned, I wouldn't have to work."

One day his supervisor came and said, "Come here, Sam." He took him to his big, plush, palatial ten-thousand-square-foot mansion. He said, "It's all yours. You can live in it; you can do whatever you want. You've got a swimming pool, a tennis court, servants--everything. Everything in this house is yours. I'm giving it to you because I don't want you to struggle with that Adam mentality. I ask only one thing: Don't lift up the box on the dining room table. Enjoy everything else in the house, be what you want to be, do your own thing, but that box on the dining room table, do not touch."

Sam said, "No problem. I can handle it." So Sam played tennis every day, went swimming, ate three meals a day. But after about five months, he saw that box. That bothered him. He wanted to know why, if he could have everything, that box was so important. He said, "No, I'm not going to touch it; I'm not going to jeopardize my time here."

After a year he had tried everything. He had gotten used to everything. There was nothing new anymore. There was only one thing new in that house, and that was that box. And so one day, when nobody was looking, he lifted up the box just a little bit. Out of that box ran a little, teeny mouse that hid, and Sam couldn't catch it and couldn't find it. The supervisor came and noted that the box had been lifted. He went to Sam and said, "Now Sam, I warned you. Go back out into the forest and pick up your ax and chop again." The next time the supervisor came by he heard Sam saying, "Oh, Sam. Oh, Sam." ᴄᴐ *Preaching Today*

THEOLOGY

In his book *LAUGHING OUT LOUD AND OTHER RELIGIOUS EXPERIENCES,* Tom Mullen tells about an engineer, a psychologist, and a theologian who were on a hunting trip in northern Canada. They knocked on the door of an isolated cabin seeking shelter and rest. The cabin was not, at the moment, occupied, but the front door was unlocked. They entered the small, two-room cabin and noticed something quite unusual. A large potbellied, cast-iron stove was suspended in mid-air by wires attached to the ceiling beams.

Why would a stove be elevated from the floor? Each of them began to look behind the phenomenon for "hidden meanings." The psychologist concluded, "It is obvious that this lonely trapper, isolated from humanity, has elevated his stove so he can curl up under it and vicariously experience a return to his mother's womb."

The engineer surmised, "The man is practicing laws of thermodynamics. By elevating his stove, he has discovered a way to distribute heat more evenly throughout the cabin."

But the theologian had a better explanation. "I'm sure that hanging his stove from the ceiling has a religious meaning. Fire lifted up has been a religious symbol for centuries."

The psychologist, the engineer, and the theologian continued their debate for some time without really resolving the issue. Finally, when the trapper returned, they immediately asked him why he had hung his potbellied stove by wires from the ceiling.

His answer was rather simple: "Had plenty of wire, not much stovepipe!" ᴄᴐ (Waco: Word Books, 1983).

And Jesus said, "Who do you say I am?" And they answered, "You are the escatological manifestation of the ground of our being, the kerygma in which we found the ultimate meaning of our interpersonal relationships." And Jesus said, "What?"

TIMIDITY

I heard about one timid little fellow who went to his first movie theater. He bought his ticket and went inside. A few minutes later he came back to the ticket office and asked for another ticket. Then he returned a third time, visibly angry, and bought another ticket. He muttered softly to the cashier, "If that man inside the door tears up my ticket one more time, I'm going home."

TRADITION

The new bridegroom looked at the results of his bride's first attempt at cooking breakfast and said glumly, "It isn't like Mom used to make."

Disappointed, she tried all the harder the next morning, producing a nicely cooked, attractive breakfast. He looked at it and muttered, "It just isn't like Mom used to make."

This went on for a number of mornings in succession. She would go to great lengths, sure she had created a tasty, well-prepared breakfast, only to be greeted with, "It isn't like Mom used to make."

Finally she became so exasperated with this cruel comment that she decided to rebel. She deliberately fried the eggs until they were hard rubber, virtually cremated the bacon, burned the toast black, and overcooked the coffee until it was almost unfit to drink.

Her husband sat down at the table, looked at the food, and beamed, "Hey! Just like Mom used to make!"

TREASURE

I enjoyed reading about a couples' club at the First United Church in Hamilton, Canada, which sponsored an annual auction sale. Everybody gathered up their accumulated junk and sent it down to the church. They brought in a professional auctioneer for the occasion. He sold all this stuff and the event raised some money for missionaries and the club budget. Well, one couple, Joe and Mildred, had some old lawn furniture that had been lying about on the veranda. Mildred thought the auction sale a marvelous opportunity to get rid of it. So she sent it all off to be sold. But when the time came for the auction, Mildred was ill and couldn't go. Joe went instead. You guessed it! Joe saw this lawn furniture and bought it. He thought he had found a terrific bargain. Poor Mildred! She had to wait another year to get rid of the stuff. ↝R. Maurice Boyd, *A Lover's Quarrel with the World,* (Philadelphia: The Westminster Press, 1985).

There was a news story that appeared recently in *USA TODAY* that might serve as a helpful parable. It seems that many McDonald's restaurants, rather than using bank bags and armored trucks, move their daily cash intake by putting the money in regular carry-out paper bags and handing the bag to a drive-thru courier. The plan conceals the fact that a large amount of money is leaving the store.

In Euclid, Ohio, though, one McDonald's store was a bit too clever. They handed the bag of concealed cash to an anonymous customer who drove up to the window to pick up his meal. For all we know he may still be anonymous--if he decided to keep the money.

TRINITY

There is a terrible story about a little girl who lived across the street from a cemetery. Often she listened to ministers speak the words of committal at the close of funeral services. She decided to have a complete funeral service of her own in her backyard. She thought she would bury her teddy bear. After digging a grave, she solemnly lowered the toy bear into the ground, saying ever so seriously the words she thought she had heard the preachers say again and again in the burial service: "In the name of the Father and of the Son and in the hole you goes!"

TRUTH

An interesting article appeared awhile back in the Clinton, SC, Chronicle titled "When The Editor Left Town." It said: "Mr. Jim Galeway and Miss Georgianne Bentlow were married Monday at the home of the bride's parents, Mr. and Mrs. Alex Bentlow, the Rev. A.A. Deckett officiating. The groom is a popular young bum who hasn't done a lick of work since he got expelled his junior year in college. He manages to dress well and keeps a supply of spending money because his dad is a soft-hearted old fool who takes up his bad checks instead of letting him go to jail where he belongs. The bride is a skinny, fast little idiot who has been kidded by every boy in town since she was 12 years old. She sucks cigarettes and drinks mean corn liquor when she is out joy-riding in her dad's car at night. She doesn't know how to cook, sew or keep house. The house was newly plastered for the wedding and the exterior newly painted, thus appropriately carrying out the decorative scheme, for the groom was newly plastered and the bride freshly painted. The groom wore a rented dinner suit over athletic underwear of imitation silk, and his pants were held up by pale green suspenders. His number 9 patent leather shoes matched his state in tightness and harmonized nicely with the axle grease polish of his hair. P.S. This is probably the last issue of this paper, but my life ambition has been to write up one wedding and tell the truth. Now that it's done, death can have no sting." ☞ Quoted by Ross W. Marrs, in *The Clergy Journal,* January, 1980, p. 22.

Former President Jimmy Carter had a reputation for honesty that was unique among politicians. In fact, that he was able to maintain this reputation was a topic of curiosity for reporters. Once, when his mother, Miss Lillian, was being interviewed by a particularly aggressive female reporter on network television, she was asked about Carter's honesty.

"Is it true," asked the reporter, "That your son doesn't lie? Can you tell me he has never told a lie?"

Miss Lillian replied, "Well, I reckon he might have told a little white lie now and then."

The reporter jumped at the opening. "I thought you said he didn't lie!" she exclaimed. "Are you telling me that white lies aren't as bad as black lies? Just what do you mean by a white lie?"

"Well," drawled Miss Lillian, "do you remember when you came in this morning and I told you how nice you looked and how glad I was to see you...?"

WOMEN

Thomas Wheeler, chief executive officer of the Massachusetts Mutual Life Insurance Company, tells a good story on himself. He says that while he and his wife were out driving he noticed they were low on gas. So he pulled off at the first exit and came to this dumpy little gas station with one pump. There was only one man working the place, so he asked the man to fill it up while he checked the oil. He added a quart of oil, closed the hood, and he saw his wife talking and smiling at the gas station attendant. When they saw him looking at them, the station attendant walked away and pretended as if nothing had happened. Wheeler paid the man and he and his wife pulled out of that seedy little station. As they drove down the road, he asked his wife if she knew the attendant. Well, she admitted she did know him. In fact, she had known him very well. For it seems that they not only had gone to high school together, but they dated seriously for about a year. Well, Wheeler couldn't help bragging a little and said, "Boy, were you lucky I came along. Because if you'd married him you'd be the wife of a gas station attendant instead of the wife of a chief executive officer." His wife replied, "My dear, if I had married him, he'd be the chief executive officer and you'd be the gas station attendant."

It's been a long, long struggle for women. This is not a recent issue. G.K. Chesterton, one of the brilliant men of the last century, pointed his great wit at the women's movement in England. He said it in a way that only Chesterton could say it, because he was a very humorous man. He said, "Ten thousand women said, 'I won't be dictated to,' and went out and became stenographers."

I was reading recently about a very noted incident in which Mr. William Collins Whitney, of the famous Vanderbilt and Whitney families, lost $85,000 at the gambling tables while waiting for his wife to dress for a party. Husbands can appreciate Mr. Whitney's predicament.

Work

We're like the lady who went to her doctor and said, "Doctor, I know I've been working too hard, but I don't want you to tell me to stop burning the candle at both ends. What I need is more wax."

George: I'd like to meet Willy.
Gracie: You can't miss him. He always wears a high collar to cover the appendicitis scar on his neck.
George: Gracie, your appendix is down on your waist.
Gracie: I know, but Willy was so ticklish they had to operate up higher.
George: What's Willy doing now?

Gracie: He just lost his job.

George: Lost his job?

Gracie: Yeah, he's a window washer.

George: And?

Gracie: And . . .he was outside on the twentieth story washing a window and when he got through he stepped back to admire his work.

George: And he lost his job. ∞Old "Burns and Allen" routine.

Somebody once asked baseball great Willie Stargell how he maintained his enthusiasm for the game. Stargell answered that he really did enjoy his job. "Have you ever heard the umpire start a game by saying, 'Work ball'?" asked Stargell. "Of course not, they always say, 'Play ball,' and that is exactly what they mean."

I heard recently about a man who applied for a job as a handyman. The prospective employer asked, "Can you do carpentry?" The man answered in the negative. "How about bricklaying?" Again the man answered, "No." The employer asked, "Well, what about electrical work?" The man said "No, I don't know anything about that either." Finally the employer said, "Well, tell me then, what is handy about you?" The man replied, "I live just around the corner."

A wealthy man in Mexico was in the habit of buying two tangerines daily from a woman who operated a tangerine stand near his house. One morning he told her that he wanted to buy her entire stock of tangerines for a party he was giving that evening. Much to his surprise the lady refused to sell him more than his customary two tangerines. "But why?" he asked with some consternation. "If I sold you all of my tangerines," she answered with dignity, "what would I do the rest of the day?"

*W*ORRY

Jess Lair reminds us about a *PEANUTS* strip in which Snoopy was having a terrible time sleeping one night. Many depressed persons can identify with his discomfort. Snoopy just couldn't sleep. He was tossing and turning on top of his doghouse wrestling with some really grave problem. Finally, about sun up, he got to sleep. Then two of the kids walked by about ten in the morning and saw Snoopy asleep. One of the kids said to his buddy, "Wouldn't it be great to be a dog and sleep all the time?" After they had gone by Snoopy just opened one eye and said, "Except at night!"

Our constant anxiety reminds me of a story that Mark Twain once told about a friend of his who came to him at the races one day and said, "I'm broke. I wish you'd buy me a ticket back to town."

Twain said, "Well, I'm pretty broke myself but, I'll tell you what to do. You hide under my seat and I'll cover you with my legs." It was agreed and Twain then went to the ticket office and bought two tickets, without saying anything to his friend. When the train was under way and the supposed stowaway was snug under the seat, the conductor came by and Twain gave him the two tickets.

"Where is the other passenger?" asked the conductor.

Twain tapped on his forehead and said in a loud voice, "That is my friend's ticket. He is a little eccentric and likes to ride under the seat." We, too, hide under the seat when we could sit out in the open and enjoy the fresh air. . .

Shalom Aleichem tells a delightful story about an old man standing on a crowded bus. The young man standing next to him asked, "What time is it?" The old man refused to reply. The young man moved on. The old man's friend, sensing something was wrong, asked, "Why were you so discourteous to the young man asking for the time?" The old man answered, "If I had given him the time of day, next he would want to know where I am going. Then we might talk about our interests. If we did that, he might invite himself to my house for dinner. If he did, he would meet my lovely daughter. If he met her, they would both fall in love. I don't want my daughter marrying someone who can't afford a watch."

Peppermint Patty, in a recent *PEANUTS* cartoon, is giving a report in school. She says, "This is my report on daytime and nighttime. Daytime is so you can see where you are going. Nighttime is so you can lie in bed and worry."

CATHY and her boyfriend are caught up in the rush of Christmas. The comic strip captions read: "*CHRISTMAS WEEK 1987!* Nerves are frayed, emotions exhausted, expectations whip around like little blizzards.

"Desperate for connection and reassurance, people turn with a whole new passion to their most solid source of security.

"Men to Monday night football. Women to the therapist!"

A housewife recently went to her doctor with complaints of feeling run down. After a thorough examination, the doctor told her, "Lady, you're not run down. You're too wound up."

Linus was talking to Charlie Brown in the comic strip *PEANUTS,* and observed: "I guess it's wrong always to be worrying about tomorrow. Maybe we should think only about today." Charlie Brown replied, "No, that's giving up. I'm still hoping that yesterday will get better."

The personnel manager of a large corporation was continually plagued over employee problems. One night while perusing the newspaper he read an article about how stress and tension drive some people to drugs. "I can understand that," he said to his wife. "I'd probably be on drugs myself if I weren't taking tranquilizers."

Sign in an office: "Frogs are smart--they eat what bugs them."

You may know the story about the truck driver who was driving through a large city. There was nothing particularly unique about the driver or the truck except for one thing--at every traffic light the driver would get out of the truck, take a baseball bat and beat on the side of the trailer at the back of the truck with all of his might. Then he would jump back in the cab of his truck and drive on to the next light where he would repeat this ritual.

A fellow following him in a car was puzzled by this bizarre behavior and asked him at one light why in the world he was beating on the side of his truck. "Oh," said the driver, "the answer is simple. I have a two-ton truck and I am carrying four tons of canaries in it. That means that I have to keep two tons of them in the air at all times."

There is the story of the man out west who went to see a psychiatrist. "Doc," he said, "I have been having these terrible dreams. One night I dreamed that I was a wigwam. The next night I was a teepee. It was awful!" The psychiatrist said, "Calm down. It's obvious that you are simply *TWO TENTS.*"

Not long ago a corporate executive came into a doctor's office for a checkup. He showed signs of overwork and stress. He was warned to slow down, to take up a hobby--perhaps painting--to relax. He readily agreed and left the office. The next day the executive phoned and announced enthusiastically, "Doc, this painting is wonderful. I've already done ten."

YOUTH

A teenager came to his pastor for advice. "I left home," said the boy, "and did something that will make my dad furious when he finds out. What should I do?"

The minister thought for a moment and replied, "Go home and confess your sin to your father, and he'll probably forgive you and treat you like the prodigal son."

Sometime later the boy reported to the minister, "Well, I told Dad what I did."

"And did he kill the fatted calf for you?" asked the minister.

"No," said the boy, "but he nearly killed the prodigal son!"

In *FUNKY WINKERBEAN,* the President addresses the graduates: "And I feel that the Class of '88 will go forth and have a very positive impact on the future! I say this in spite of the misgivings I had when I saw in the yearbook that the person you most admired was Fred Flintstone."

In the cartoon *FOR BETTER OR WORSE,* Michael's mother attended the school open house night and met his teacher.

Teacher: "Mrs. Patterson? Michael's Mother? I'm so very pleased to meet you. I must say that your Michael is a delight to have in my class! He's helpful, conscientious, courteous. . ."

Michael's mother gets a peculiar look on her face and thinks: "My kid? She was talking about *MY* kid?"

Then she runs into her son: "Michael, your teacher says that your behaviour is excellent at school. Why can't you be that good at home?"

Michael replies, scratching his head: "Mom, I've only got so much goodness to go around!"

Teenagers anxious to meet others can now dial *GABB*, *BLAB*, Connections, Rapline, or any of the dozens of other "party lines" currently providing teens a chance to talk to others. For a fee, you can call and talk to up to ten people at a time.

So what do they talk about? The description of one's appearance is a major topic of conversation. One writer who participated in several calls to learn what purpose these lines served recorded several conversations. He heard one girl describe herself thus: "You know the girl in that video for that song? I look like her twin. So if you want to see what I look like, watch that video."

A boy's response to a female caller's question about his appearance was, "Like a cross between Rob Lowe and Sylvester Stallone."

But a much more detailed description ensued on the junior version of the Connections line to be used by callers up to 15 years old. One male caller described his looks: "I'm 6'tall, I weigh 170, my hair's like Brian Bosworth's, and I have a black Chevy."

The girl listening replied, "Neat!"

Then another line was picked up. A much younger male voice came on the line. "First, he's not 6' tall. Second, his hair's not like Brian Bosworth's, and third, he doesn't have a car!"

The girl laughed, and they hung up. ∞ "The Children's Hour" by Bob Greene in *Esquire,* May 1988 and "Dial-a-Date/With No Hang-Ups" in *Newsweek* May 30, 1988.

Charles Turkington tells about seeing a classified ad in the newspaper during the 1960s, the time when a lot of young people were running away from home and joining communes. The ad was placed by the father of a teenaged son who had run away from home. Here's how the ad ran:

"Sheldon, Come home. Stop chasing flowers and hippies. True values can be found only at home. When you're ready to come back, let me know because we rented your room. Papa"

Calvin Miller in an article in *LEADERSHIP* writes about a rule he had for his daughter Melanie that she could not date until she was sixteen. At fifteen and three-fourths, the Christmas Dance came along and a boy asked her to go. When he stood firm, she became incensed and said, "Dad, I just hope that the Lord comes back between now and February so you have to live with yourself through eternity knowing that I never had a date!"